Soccer Training

This book is dedicated to Gene (Geno) Klein, a great friend and outstanding coach. He is missed by all who had the pleasure of knowing him.

Joseph Luxbacher

Foreword by Chris Karwoski

SOCCER TRAINING

160 Drills to Develop Skills and Tactics for Players Ages 10-18

Meyer & Meyer Sport

British Library of Cataloguing in Publication Data
A catalogue record for this book is available from the British Library

Soccer Training
Maidenhead: Meyer & Meyer Sport (UK) Ltd., 2025
ISBN: 978-1-78255-272-7

Aachen, Auckland, Beirut, Cairo, Cape Town, Dubai, Hägendorf, Hong Kong, Indianapolis, Maidenhead, Manila, New Delhi, Singapore, Sydney, Tehran, Vienna

Member of the World Sport Publishers' Association (WSPA), www.w-s-p-a.org

Printed by Versa Press, East Peoria, IL
Printed in the United States of America

Credits
Cover and interior design: Anja Elsen
Layout: DiTech Publishing Services, www.ditechpubs.com
Cover photo: © AdobeStock
Interior figures: Easy Sports Graphics, sports-graphics.com
Managing editor: Elizabeth Evans
Copy editor: Anne Rumery

ISBN: 978-1-78255-272-7
Email: info@m-m-sports.com
www.thesportspublisher.com

CONTENTS

FOREWORD

As a coach with more than 30 years of experience at all competitive levels, I can attest that this compilation of soccer training exercises by Dr. Joseph Luxbacher is a valuable resource for both aspiring soccer coaches and the players under their charge. Coach Luxbacher's knowledge of and experience in the world's most popular game is clearly evident in his latest book, which includes a variety of exercises that cover all aspects of soccer training: dynamic warm-ups, technical (skill) progressions, and individual and group tactical concepts. I frequently share these drills and exercises with coaches and players of the various age group teams playing for the FC Pittsburgh Soccer Club, where I am the Boys Director of Coaching.

Appropriate for and adaptable to players of various ages, experience, and ability levels, the content presented in Soccer Training provides coaches and players alike with clear and detailed explanations on the setup, objectives, and procedure of each exercise, facilitating consistent application at all levels of coaching. Coach Luxbacher's thorough coverage of the essential elements required for the training and progressive development of the modern player provides specific insights into advanced coaching methodologies in a clear and concisely presented format.

I enthusiastically endorse Coach Luxbacher's approach to training and developing young soccer players. Using these drills and exercises highlights the technical and tactical concepts that form the foundation for modern player development. I highly recommend this book to fellow coaches, interested parents, and anyone involved in teaching the game to young players.

–Chris Karwoski

PA West Assistant Classic League Director

Director of Operations and Boys Director of Coaching – FC Pittsburgh Soccer Club

Head Men's Coach – LaRoche University

PREFACE

Internationally known as football, soccer is the world's most popular game, the major sport of nearly every country in Asia, Africa, Europe, and South America. According to the **Fédération internationale de football association (FIFA)**, the governing body of international soccer, there are more than 250 million players, in addition to 5 million referees and officials, actively involved in the game today. Soccer remains the only football-type game played at the Olympics, and millions more people follow the men's World Cup tournament, soccer's international championship, than follow the National Football League (NFL) Super Bowl and Major League Baseball (MLB) World Series. The 2022 World Cup final between Argentina and France broke several TV audience records in key international markets. An in-home audience of nearly 1.5 billion people watched the game live on television and were witness to a thrilling exhibition of sporting drama as Argentina defeated defending world champion France in a penalty shootout after a 3-3 draw in Qatar.

Soccer's universal appeal does not rest with it being an easy game to play successfully. In fact, soccer may demand more of its players, both physically and mentally, than any other sport. The game is played on the largest field of any sport except polo (where horses do the bulk of the work!). Players must perform a variety of passing, dribbling, and shooting foot skills while under the match pressures of restricted space, limited time, physical fatigue, and determined opponents challenging for the ball. There are no official time-outs during a typical 90-minute match and substitution is limited. A thorough understanding of tactics and strategies is also requisite for successful performance at the highest levels of competition where decision-making skills are constantly tested as players respond to ever-changing situations during play.

Except for the goalkeeper there are no specialists on the soccer field. Each player is required to play a role in team defense when their opponents are in possession of the ball, and conversely must contribute to the attack when their team has possession of the ball. The game demands a high level of fitness, skill, and athleticism from all participants. Field players may run several miles during a 90-minute match with much of that distance at sprint-like intensity. The physical and mental challenges confronting players are many and varied. Individual and team performance ultimately depends on each player's ability to successfully meet these challenges.

As millions of young players embrace the sport with every passing year, there is an increased need for knowledgeable coaches, leaders, and teachers who can provide a positive learning environment for the players under their charge. This book has been written with that goal in mind—to provide coaches and parents with information that will enable them to provide young players with the best possible soccer experience.

ACKNOWLEDGMENTS

The writing and publishing of a book truly requires a team effort. In that regard I am deeply indebted to an outstanding team of individuals for their help and support with this project. Although it is not possible to mention everyone by name, I would like to express my deepest appreciation to the following individuals: to my beautiful wife Gail, the love of my life, for her willingness to trade personal time for writing time as the deadlines drew near; to Liz Evans, editor at Meyer & Meyer, for her insight, patience, and support in the development of this book; and to the many players and coaches who were willing to share thoughts and ideas.

INTRODUCTION

MAKE SOCCER TRAINING: 160 DRILLS TO DEVELOP SKILLS AND TACTICS FOR PLAYERS AGES 10–18 WORK FOR YOU

Planning practices that challenge players—training sessions that keep them active, interested, and involved—is a fundamental responsibility of the soccer coach. Soccer players of all ages and ability levels, and particularly young players, want to be excited, enthused, and have fun while they work to improve their game. They will not respond well to long-winded lectures, standing in long lines waiting for an infrequent opportunity to touch the ball, or anything else that spells boredom. Young aspiring soccer players will derive the most benefit from practices that are action oriented, from drills that require them to be constantly moving, touching the ball, and scoring goals.

Soccer Training was written with that goal in mind. The book contains a variety of game-related exercises that can be used to create a rich and varied practice environment. The drills contained in each section focus on mastery of the skills and tactics required to become a more complete soccer player. Most drills are appropriate for novice and intermediate-level players, and with a few minor adjustments can be adjusted to match the ability and experience of older, more accomplished players. For example, coaches can make a simple possession drill more challenging by doing the following:

- Impose restrictions on players; for example, require one- or two-touch passes only.

- Adjust the size of the playing area (reducing the area increases the degree of difficulty since players must perform the same skills with less time and with less space).

- Increase the physical demands by requiring more running and player movement.

- Include the ultimate challenge—the pressure of determined opponents competing for the ball.

Each drill is organized and described as follows:

Title. For most drills the title provides a general idea of its primary focus. For example, the drill "Shoot Off of the Dribble" requires players to dribble at speed and release a shot on goal. Some drill titles are not as obvious, however, and the coach can look to the other headings, such as *Objectives*, for more information on the drill utility.

Objectives. Most drills have a primary objective and one or more closely associated secondary objectives. For example, the primary objective of the drill titled "Knockout" is the development of dribbling skills used to possess and protect the ball in tight spaces. Secondary objectives include the development of shielding and tackling skills, as well as an improved level of fitness. By utilizing drills that accomplish more than one objective, coaches can make the most efficient use of practice time.

Setup. Field dimensions, equipment required, number of players involved, and any other special needs are listed under this heading. Balls, cones, flags, and colored scrimmage vests are some of the more commonly used equipment items. Field dimensions are provided only as general guidelines, and should be adjusted to the age, number, and ability of players.

Procedure. This section provides a brief overview of how the drill is played (e.g., rules, restrictions). In some drills coaches may be involved as servers/ passers while observing the action, although that is not always the case. Most drills are structured so that players can organize the action and get play started.

Coaching Tips. Suggestions are provided to help coaches provide corrective feedback to the players. When appropriate, safety and liability concerns are also addressed.

The book is organized into sections, each dealing with a specific skill set or aspect of the game. **Section 1** provides a variety of warm-up activities designed to prepare players, both physically and mentally, for more vigorous training to follow. **Sections 2 through 7** provide drills that focus on the improvement of specific skills or tactical concepts. Although drills are categorized based upon the primary skill emphasized, most actually involve two or more fundamental skills. For example, the drills described in **Section 6 (Individual and Group Tactics)** require players to perform a variety of skills while making split-seconds decisions such as whether to pass, dribble, or shoot the ball in a specific situation. As a result, players can derive fitness, skill, and tactical benefits all within the same exercise.

When planning practice sessions coaches should select drills most appropriate for the age and ability of the players involved. Expose novice players to more basic drills so that they are challenged but can also achieve some degree of success. Beginner level drills focus primarily on technique (skill) development. Most are competitive and involve multiple repetitions of the specific skill. As players become more competent, coaches can include drills that replicate actual game-simulated tactical situations. Such drills place an increased emphasis on speed of play and quick decision-making under the pressure of challenging opponents. Experienced players will derive greater benefit from drills that mirror the conditions they face in actual match situations.

PLANNING PRACTICE SESSIONS

Keep in mind that young soccer players are not miniature adults, so a practice designed for a college-aged team may be completely inappropriate for an under 10-year-old group. Select drills that challenge players to achieve a higher standard but are not beyond their ability to perform successfully. In short, place players in training situations where they have a realistic opportunity to experience success.

The following general guidelines can be applied to players of all ages and ability levels and are provided to assist in planning practice sessions. These guidelines are suggestions only and should be adjusted to accommodate the specific needs and abilities of the group.

1. Create a Positive Learning Environment.

Keep players active, involved, and touching the ball as often as possible. Training sessions should be challenging but also provide an enjoyable experience for players and coaches alike.

2. Plan Each Practice Session Around a Central Theme.

Structure each practice around a series of drills and small-sided games related to a central theme, for example, the improvement of passing and receiving skills.

Do not attempt to cover too many topics in a single practice, particularly with younger players.

3. Ensure a Safe Practice Environment.

A safe practice environment should include the following:

- proper planning and organization,
- adequate supervision,
- matching players with others of similar size and ability,
- establishing guidelines for appropriate behavior, and
- soccer goals securely anchored.

4. Conduct a Player-Centered Practice.

Use brief demonstrations and simple explanations, and get players actively involved as quickly as possible. The less time players stand around the more productive the practice.

5. Consider a Player's Soccer Age.

A player's soccer age refers to their level of competence and may differ significantly from chronological age. Novice players may have difficulty performing even the most fundamental skills, so coaches should not place them in situations where they have little or no chance of achieving some degree of success. Plan a realistic practice, one that challenges players but is within their physical and mental capabilities.

6. Avoid Long Lines and Long Lectures.

The more times a player can pass, receive, shoot, or dribble the ball, the more likely he or she will enjoy the practice and improve their skill level. Avoid long lines with players waiting their turn for an infrequent opportunity to touch the ball. Short lines, brief instructions, and constant activity are advised. An adequate supply of balls should be available, ideally one for each player, Feedback should be positive and to the point!

7. Keep It Simple.

Complicated drills or training exercises will confuse and frustrate rather than motivate players. All successful coaches adhere to the **KISS principle**—*Keep It Simple, Stupid!*

8. Take It Step by Step.

Each drill should lay the groundwork for those that follow. Introduce the practice with basic activities and progress to more match-like situations. Where to start in the progression depends upon the ability and experience of the players involved. Higher-level, more experienced players should naturally begin practice with more challenging exercises than would novice players.

9. Conclude each practice with a game or game-simulated exercise.

Small-sided games (3 vs 3 up to 6 vs 6) are beneficial in many respects. Playing with fewer numbers than a full-sided game allows players greater opportunity to pass, dribble, and shoot at goal. Small-sided games require players to make more decisions as they are directly involved in virtually every play, a situation which promotes tactical development. Emphasis on positional play is also reduced in small-sided games because each player must defend as well as attack, a situation that promotes total player development.

SECTION 1
WARM-UP ACTIVITIES

Players should undergo a warm-up prior to each training session and match. Warm-up activities serve the important function of preparing players, both physically and mentally, for more vigorous activity by increasing muscle temperatures, promoting increased blood flow, improving reflex time, and minimizing next-day soreness. Warm-up activities should be of sufficient intensity and duration to induce sweating, an indicator that muscle temperatures have elevated. This process can take anywhere from 15 to 30 minutes, depending on the ambient temperature, humidity, and general environmental conditions.

Most players and coaches generally prefer warm-up activities that are soccer-specific; in other words, related to playing the game of soccer. A soccer-specific warm-up consists of activities that involve the actual skills, movements, and mobility required of players in a soccer match. The warm-up drills described in this section are intended to provide a variety of options for team (group) warm-up while preparing players for the physical challenges to follow.

DRIBBLE IN, PASS OUT

OBJECTIVE

- Warm-up activity leading into a training session that focuses on passing and receiving skills

SETUP

- Play within the center circle (or similarly sized area of the field).

- Three or four players are positioned inside the circle, each with a soccer ball.

- The remaining players spread themselves along the perimeter of the circle.

- Players on the perimeter of the circle do not have a ball.

PROCEDURE

1. On the coach command, players dribble freely within the circle, avoiding all other dribblers.

2. At their discretion the dribblers pass their ball to a teammate of their choice positioned along the perimeter of the circle and switch places with that player.

3. The player receiving the ball uses their first touch on the ball to take them inside the circle where they are free to dribble and at their discretion pass to a teammate stationed along the perimeter of the circle and switch places with that player.

4. Continue the dribble-in and pass-out activity for 10 minutes at a high pace.

COACHING TIPS

*   This warm-up activity is appropriate for almost any age group.

*   Players can work to improve their first touch, dribbling, and passing skills.

DRIBBLE FREEZE TAG

OBJECTIVE

*   To improve dribbling skills when performing in restricted space and with limited time to make decisions

SETUP

*   Position markers to create a playing area 20 yards square.

*   Each player has possession of a ball except for two players who are designated as the taggers.

*   The taggers position themselves outside of the area to begin.

*   All other players, each with a ball, position within the area.

PROCEDURE

1. Players begin to dribble randomly within the area, keeping close control of their ball.

2. On coach command, the taggers enter the area to chase after and tag the dribblers.

3. Dribblers who are tagged are frozen and must stand stationary with one foot on the ball.

4. A player can be unfrozen by a teammate who dribbles near and tags her or him.

5. Play for two minutes or until all dribblers are frozen, then change taggers and repeat.

COACHING TIPS

- Encourage the use of dribbling maneuvers coupled with sudden changes in speed and direction while maintaining close control of the ball.

3 STATION WARM-UP

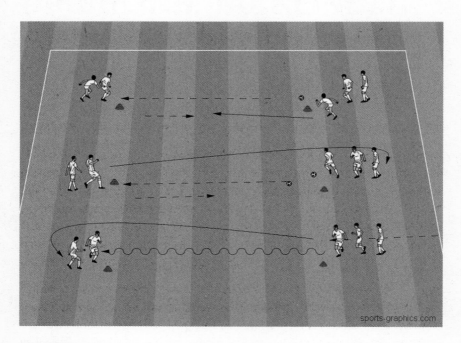

sports-graphics.com

OBJECTIVE

- To prepare players for a training session focused on passing and dribbling skills

SETUP

- Divide the team into groups of four to six players.

- Place two markers 15 to 20 yards apart for each group.

- For each group, two or three players are positioned at opposite markers facing one another.

- One (1) ball is required per group.

PROCEDURE

1. Perform three 5-minute stations.

2. **Station 1.** The player with the ball dribbles to the opposite line of players, exchanges the ball with the first player in that line, and remains there. The player receiving the ball does likewise in the opposite direction.

3. **Station 2.** The player with the ball passes to the first player in the opposite line and follows the pass to that group. Receiving player does likewise in the opposite direction.

4. **Station 3.** Double Pass Combination (*for more advanced players*). The player with the ball passes to the first player in the opposite line, moves forward to receive a return pass, and then passes the ball to the next player in the opposite line who repeats process in the opposite direction. ** *Players follow their pass to the end of the opposite line.* **

COACHING TIPS

*   Encourage players to use only two touches, if possible, to receive and pass the ball (first touch to prepare, second touch to pass).

HIT OR MISS

OBJECTIVE

- To rehearse passing and dribbling skills in a large group warm-up exercise

SETUP

- Mark off an area of 20 by 25 yards.

- Require that a ball be available for each player as needed.

- Three players (**passers**) begin with possession of a ball and are positioned along the perimeter of the area.

- Place remaining balls outside the area.

- Players without a ball (**dodgers**) scatter throughout the grid area.

PROCEDURE

1. On the coach command the **passers** dribble into the grid and attempt to pass their ball so that it contacts **dodgers** below the knees.

2. Passers must use the inside of the foot for all passes–*shooting is not permitted!*

3. The dodgers use sudden changes in speed and direction to avoid being hit by a passed ball.

4. A dodger who is contacted below the knees with a passed ball collects a ball from the extra balls placed outside the area and joins the passers.

5. Play continues until there are only three dodgers remaining.

6. Those players become passers for the next round.

COACHING TIPS

- This exercise requires players to dribble and get their heads up to make a pass.

- Adjust the area size to match the age, passing ability, and number of players involved.

GROUP PASS OR DRIBBLE

OBJECTIVE

- To rehearse passing and dribbling skills in a warm-up exercise

SETUP

- Divide the group into two teams of equal numbers.

- Designate one team as the **passing team**, and the other as the **dribbling team**.

- Play within a 30-yard square area.

- The passing team has possession of one ball.

- Each player on the dribbling team has possession of a ball.

PROCEDURE

1. **Dribbling** team players dribble randomly within the area while maintaining close control of their ball and performing various dribbling moves.

2. At the same time, **passing team** players circulate a ball among themselves as they move throughout the area.

3. **Passing team** players should avoid contacting dribblers with a passed ball.

4. After 5–6 minutes of continuous play, teams switch roles and repeat.

COACHING TIPS

- All players should be in constant movement (dribbling or passing) throughout the entire warm-up period.

MINNOWS AND SHARKS

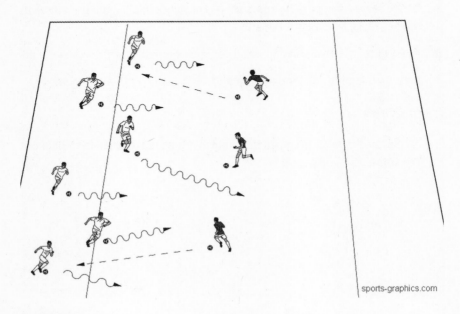

sports-graphics.com

OBJECTIVE

• To incorporate passing and dribbling skills in a group warm-up activity

SETUP

• Use markers to outline a channel area 20 yards wide by 30 yards long with a safety zone 3 yards deep at each end.

• Station three **sharks** in the center of the channel, each with a ball.

• The remaining players **(i.e., minnows)**, each with a ball, are stationed in the safety zone on one end of the field facing the sharks.

PROCEDURE

1. On coach command, the minnows attempt to dribble the length of the channel past the sharks to the opposite safety zone.

2. Sharks can capture minnows by contacting them below the knees with a passed ball.

3. All passes must be made with the inside or outside surface of the foot; *no shooting is permitted*.

4. A minnow contacted below the knees with a passed ball is considered captured and joins the sharks for the next round.

5. Minnows who reach the opposite safety zone without being contacted with a passed ball remain there until the coach issues the command to return to the original safety zone.

6. Minnows dribble back and forth between safety zones until all but three have been captured.

7. These three players are sharks to begin the next round.

COACHING TIPS

• Encourage minnows to use sudden changes of speed and/or direction when dribbling to evade the sharks.

HUNT THE RABBIT

sports-graphics.com

OBJECTIVE

- To rehearse the movement patterns required to create passing combinations to maintain possession of the ball

SETUP

- Play within an area 40 yards square.

- Split the group into two teams of equal numbers. Both teams are positioned within the area.

- Use colored scrimmage vests to differentiate teams.

- Designate one player on each team as a **rabbit** who wears distinctive clothing (e.g., hat, vest).

- Each team has possession of a ball.

PROCEDURE

1. Passing among teammates is accomplished by **throwing and catching—not kicking**—the ball.

2. A team scores a goal by quickly circulating (by throwing and catching) the ball among teammates to get in position to hit the opposing rabbit below the knees with a thrown ball.

3. The rabbit is free to move anywhere within the area to avoid being hit.

4. Players are permitted 6 or fewer steps with the ball before releasing it to a teammate or throwing at the rabbit.

5. Teammates can protect their rabbit by blocking opponents' throws.

6. Change of possession occurs when a pass is intercepted by a member of the opposing team, when the ball drops to the ground, or when a player takes more than six steps without releasing the ball.

7. Two balls are in play at all times.

8. The first team to score three goals wins the game.

COACHING TIPS

- Encourage players to continually adjust their position to provide multiple passing (tossing) options for the teammate with the ball.

- Repeat the game several times with different players serving as the rabbits.

FILL THE BUCKET

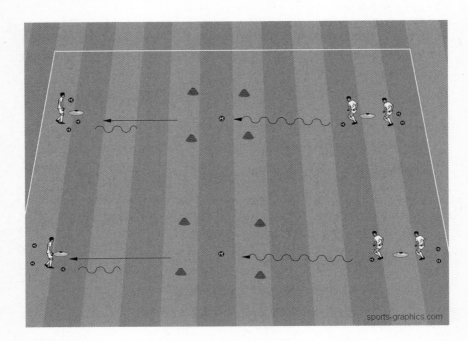

OBJECTIVE

• To practice dribbling skills in a competitive fun-filled exercise

SETUP

• Organize teams of three players each.

For each team:

• Position two markers 30 yards apart.

• Place three balls at each end marker.

• Position four additional markers to outline a 5-yard square (the bucket) midway between the end markers.

• Two players are positioned at one end marker and the third player is positioned at the opposite end marker.

PROCEDURE

1. On the coach command "go," the first player (in the line of two) dribbles at top speed and deposits a ball in the bucket.

2. After doing so, the player continues running to the opposite end marker and tags the teammate stationed there.

3. The tagged player repeats the process in the opposite direction.

4. Continue until all six balls are deposited in the bucket.

5. The first team to deposit all six of the balls in the bucket wins the competition.

COACHING TIPS

•   Players should dribble at top speed and slow down as they enter the bucket to deposit their ball.

CHAIN TAG

OBJECTIVE

- To improve player mobility, agility, and fitness

SETUP

- Play within an area of approximately 30 yards square.

- Designate two players as "it" who are stationed outside the area.

- All remaining free players position themselves within the area.

- Soccer balls are not required.

PROCEDURE

1. The two players who are "it" enter the area to chase and tag free players.

2. Free players are permitted to move anywhere within the area to avoid being tagged.

3. A free player who is tagged must join hands with the "it" player who tagged him or her to form a chain.

4. As additional players are tagged the chains grow longer.

5. Only two chains are permitted at any time. The original chains may not split into smaller chains.

6. Chains can work together to corner or trap free players.

7. Continue until only two free players remain.

8. Repeat the game with those two players designated as "it" to begin the next round.

COACHING TIPS

•   Vary the size of the area depending upon the number of players.

•   Encourage players to use sudden changes of speed and direction coupled with deceptive body feints to avoid being tagged.

HUNT A NEW BALL

OBJECTIVE

- To practice dribbling maneuvers in a group warm-up activity

SETUP

- Use markers to outline an area of 30 yards square.

- All players, each with a ball, position themselves within the area.

PROCEDURE

1. Players dribble randomly throughout the playing area, keeping close control of the ball and avoiding contact with other players.

2. On the coach command *"exchange*," each player steps on their ball to stop it, then quickly leaves their ball to find a new one, and immediately begin dribbling again.

3. The coach repeats the "exchange" command every 20–30 seconds.

4. Continue for 8–10 minutes nonstop.

COACHING TIPS

•   Encourage players to dribble at a rapid pace for the entire warm-up exercise.

TOSS, CATCH, AND SCORE

OBJECTIVES

- To simulate the support movement patterns used in actual match situations
- To improve fitness
- To foster an enthusiastic training mentality

SETUP

- Play on one half of a regulation field.
- Position a goal at each end line of the field.
- Divide the group into two teams.
- Use colored vests to differentiate teams.

- One ball is required per game.

- Do not use goalkeepers.

PROCEDURE

1. Each team defends a goal and can score in the opponent's goal.

2. Regular soccer rules apply, except that players pass and receive the ball by throwing and catching rather than kicking the ball.

3. Players may take up to five steps with the ball before releasing (passing) it to a teammate or throwing (shooting) at the goal.

4. Change of possession occurs when the ball drops to the ground, a pass is intercepted, or a goal is scored.

5. Players are not permitted to wrestle the ball from an opponent.

6. Although there are no designated goalkeepers, all players are permitted to use their hands to block opponents' shots at goal.

7. A goal is scored by throwing the ball into the opponent's goal. The team scoring the most goals wins the match.

COACHING TIPS

- Encourage player movement to find a position at the proper angle and distance to provide passing options for the player with the ball.

PREDATOR OR PREY

OBJECTIVES

- To rehearse dribbling skills in a warm-up activity

- To improve player agility and mobility

SETUP

- Play within an area of 30 yards square.

- Position markers to designate a safety zone of 5 yards square at each corner of the field.

- Designate two **predators** who position themselves in the center of the playing area (without soccer balls).

- Divide remaining players (**prey**), each with soccer ball, into four groups.

- Position a group in each of the four safety zones.

PROCEDURE

1. On the coach's command **"Begin the Hunt,"** the drill begins.

2. Players (prey) stationed in the safety zones must dribble to another safety zone before being tagged by a predator.

3. If a player dribbles to another safety zone without being tagged he or she can briefly rest there but may only remain in that zone for 20 seconds or less before attempting to dribble to a different safety zone.

4. A player who is tagged becomes a predator.

5. The original predator takes the ball and becomes prey.

COACHING TIPS

- To make the drill more difficult for predators, the prey can place a colored scrimmage vest hanging out of their shorts and require the predators to pull the vest out rather than simply tag the prey.

CAPTURE THE FLAG

OBJECTIVES

- To practice dribbling skills in a confined area

- To evade an opponent challenging for the ball through sudden changes of speed and direction while maintaining close control of the ball

SETUP

- Use markers to outline an area of 25 yards square.

- Designate two players as defenders who are stationed outside of the area.

- All other players, each with a ball, position themselves within the area.

- Each player tucks a colored scrimmage vest (i.e., the flag), into the back of his or her shorts so that it hangs out.

PROCEDURE

1. All players begin dribbling in random fashion within the square.

2. On the coach command, the two defenders sprint into the area to chase the dribblers and pull (capture) the flag from their shorts.

3. Dribblers use sudden changes of speed, direction, or both to evade the chasing defenders.

4. If a dribbler's flag is captured, he or she immediately becomes a defender and attempts to steal another dribbler's flag.

5. The original defender who captures a flag tucks it in his or her shorts and becomes a dribbler.

6. Dribblers must maintain close control of their ball as they try to evade the defenders.

COACHING TIPS

- Encourage dribblers to keep their head up as much as possible to ensure maximum field vision.

REDS TO BLUES, BLUES TO REDS

OBJECTIVE

*   To rehearse passing and receiving skills in a group warm-up exercise

SETUP

*   Play within one half of the field.

*   Divide the group into two teams of five to eight players each.

*   Teams wear different colored scrimmage vests (blues, reds).

*   Each team starts with possession of three or four balls.

PROCEDURE

1. On coach command, players from both teams begin moving throughout the field area.

2. Those with a ball dribble, while those without a ball move into areas where they can receive a pass from an opposing player (**reds pass to blues, blues pass to reds**).

3. All players should be in continuous motion throughout the warm-up exercise.

4. Two restrictions are placed on players: passes must be on the ground, and players with a ball must only pass to a player on the opposite team.

COACHING TIPS

- Encourage players to receive and control the ball into the space of their next movement.

- As the ball is received it should not be stopped completely but rather controlled into the space away from an imaginary defender.

TAKE IT OR LEAVE IT

sports-graphics.com

OBJECTIVE

• To rehearse the takeover maneuver (ball exchange) with a teammate

SETUP

• Position markers to outline an area of 30 yards square.

• All players are positioned within the area.

• One ball should be available for every two players.

PROCEDURE

1. All players move randomly throughout the playing area. Those with a ball dribble, while those without a ball jog at three-quarter speed.

2. At the coach's command, the dribblers exchange their ball with a teammate who does not have possession of a ball using the standard takeover maneuver.

3. Players should perform the **same foot** takeover maneuver—for example, when a player is dribbling directly at a teammate and has the ball on the right foot, the teammate who is performing the takeover should take the ball with the right foot.

4. The same procedure applies when the ball is on the left foot.

COACHING TIPS

*   Teammates should communicate with each other through verbal signals or subtle body movements.

*   When executing the same foot takeover maneuver, the player with the ball should dribble directly at a teammate while controlling the ball with the foot farthest (on the opposite side) from an imaginary defender.

*   As players cross paths they exchange possession of the ball right foot to right foot, or left foot to left foot.

*   To make the game more difficult, add one or two passive defenders to the exercise.

FOX HUNT

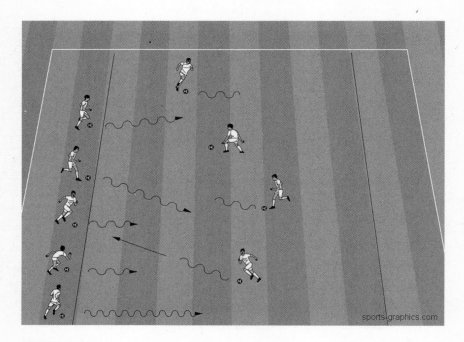

sports-graphics.com

OBJECTIVES

- To rehearse passing and dribbling skills in a warm-up activity

- To improve player mobility, agility, and fitness

SETUP

- Use markers to outline an area 30 yards in length and 25 yards in width with a safety zone 5 yards deep at each end.

- Designate three players as huntsmen who are positioned in the center of the field, each with a ball.

- All remaining players (foxes), each with a ball, station themselves in a safety zone facing the marksmen.

PROCEDURE

1. On command, the foxes attempt to dribble the length of the area into the opposite safety zone.

2. Huntsmen can capture a fox by contacting the dribbler below the knees with a passed ball.

3. All passes must be made with the inside or outside surface of the foot. Instep shooting is *not* permitted.

4. A fox contacted below the knees with a passed ball is considered captured and joins the huntsmen for the next round.

5. Foxes who reach the opposite safety zone remain there until the coach issues the command to return to the original safety zone.

6. Foxes dribble from one safety zone to the other on the coach command until all but three have been captured. These players are huntsmen for the next round.

COACHING TIPS

- Encourage huntsmen to dribble close to their targets before passing the ball.

- Adjust the area size to match the ages, abilities, and number of players involved.

CALL A MEDIC

OBJECTIVE

- To incorporate dribbling, running, and fitness in a group warm-up activity

SETUP

- Place markers to outline a playing area of about 50 yards square.

- Divide the group into three teams of equal number.

- Position markers to designate a 10-by-10-yard safety zone for each team in a corner of the playing area.

- All players, each with a ball, station themselves within their team's safety square.

- Each team designates one of its members as the team medic who wears a distinctive colored vest.

- The team medic is also stationed within the team safety zone but is without a ball.

PROCEDURE

1. On the coach command "go," all players dribble out of their home safety zone to chase after players from other teams.

2. The objective is to chase opponents and contact them beneath the knees with a passed ball while at the same time avoiding being hit below the knees by an opponents' pass.

3. Any player contacted with a passed ball is frozen and must take a knee at that spot.

4. Frozen players can be released (unfrozen) by their team medic who must leave the team's safety square to tag frozen teammates.

5. The medic does not have to dribble a ball.

6. After being tagged by their team medic, frozen players are released to continue dribbling after opponents.

7. The team medic is safe when he or she is within the teams' safety square but can be contacted with a passed ball from an opponent when outside of the safety square.

8. If a medic is contacted with a ball when attempting to unfreeze teammates, he or she is permanently frozen and from that point on players from that team who are frozen cannot be released.

9. Play a series of 5-minute games.

10. The team that has the fewest players frozen after 5 minutes wins the game.

COACHING TIPS

- Reduce the area size for younger players to make it easier for players to hit their chosen targets.

NUTMEG RACES

sports-graphics.com

OBJECTIVES

- To practice sudden changes of speed and direction while dribbling the ball
- To maintain close control of the ball when dribbling in a confined area

SETUP

- Divide the group into two teams of equal numbers (team 1 and team 2).
- Use markers to outline a playing area of 30 yards square.
- Team 1 positions themselves as stationary targets with feet spread apart at various spots within the playing area.
- Team 2, each with a ball, position themselves outside the area.

PROCEDURE

1. On the coach's command, team 2 players dribble into the area and attempt to push their balls through the legs of as many team 1 players as possible during a 60-second round.

2. The dribbling maneuver of pushing the ball through an opponent's legs is referred to as a **nutmeg** and, in actual game play, is the ultimate embarrassment for a defender.

3. Team 1 players must remain stationary with feet spread apart during the 60-second round.

4. A dribbler is not permitted to nutmeg the same opponent twice in succession.

5. Teams reverse roles for the next round and for each successive round.

6. Play at least six rounds.

7. Players keep total of how many nutmegs they perform in each 60-second round.

8. Teammates total their scores after each round.

9. The team with the most nutmegs after six rounds wins the competition.

COACHING TIPS

-   Encourage players to complete as many nutmegs as possible in 60 seconds.

-   Dribblers should keep close control of the ball as they move from one nutmeg target to the next.

SECTION 2
DRIBBLING, TACKLING, AND SHIELDING SKILLS

Similar to the sport of basketball, dribbling skills are used primarily to maintain possession of the ball while running past opponents or when advancing with the ball in open space. Effective dribbling skills potentially enable a player to penetrate an opposing defensive block and as such can play an important role in a successful team attack. On the flip side, excessive dribbling at inopportune times or in inappropriate areas of the field will disrupt the collective team play required to create quality scoring opportunities.

Dribbling in soccer is sometimes referred to as an art rather than a skill because there is simply not one standard method of dribbling. Players are free to develop their own dribbling style so long as it achieves the primary objectives. The ways in which players incorporate various movements and maneuvers into their personal dribbling style can vary. In essence, if a dribbling maneuver works for you, then by all means use it.

In general, players can use dribbling skills to best advantage in the attacking half of the field nearest to the opponent's goal, an area where the **risk** of possession loss by dribbling is counterbalanced by the potential **reward** of creating a goal scoring opportunity. Players should limit dribbling—particularly dribbling to take on opponents—when in their teams' half of the field, an area where the risk of possession loss is greater than the potential reward of bypassing an opponent on the dribble. Young players should be coached to recognize situations where dribbling can be used to their advantage.

Two general dribbling styles are commonly observed in game situations. Players use short, choppy steps coupled with deceptive changes of speed and direction when attempting to bypass (penetrate past) an opponent. Conversely, when advancing in open space speed becomes more of a priority than close control of the ball. In that situation players do not keep the ball so tight to their feet but instead push it ahead several strides, usually with the outside surface of the instep, sprint to it, and then push it again.

Shielding is the technique used to protect the ball from an opponent who is attempting to gain possession. To shield the ball, the dribbler positions their body between the ball and the challenging opponent and controls the ball with the foot farthest from the opponent.

Tackling is a purely defensive skill used to gain possession of the ball from an opponent. Three different techniques—the block tackle, poke tackle, and slide tackle—are commonly used, depending on the situation. The block tackle is the preferred technique to use when an opponent is dribbling directly at a defender. The poke and slide tackles are typically used when a defender is approaching the dribbler from the side or from behind. The block tackle has several advantages over the poke and slide tackles. First and foremost, it allows for greater body control and enables the defender to initiate a counterattack once gaining possession of the ball. In addition, if the defending player fails to win the ball, then he or she is still in position to recover and chase after the opponent.

The drills described in this section emphasize the development of dribbling, shielding, and tackling skills, often within the same exercise. Most also provide the added benefit of fitness training because players are moving continuously throughout the drills.

FOLLOW THE LEADER

OBJECTIVE

- To improve dribbling skills

SETUP

- Play within an area of approximately 25 yards square.

- Each player pairs with a partner and stations themselves within the area.

- A soccer ball is required for each player.

- Designate one partner as the leader, and the other as the follower.

PROCEDURE

1. On the coach command, the leader dribbles randomly within the area while the partner closely follows.

2. The leader constantly varies the pace and direction of the dribble pattern.

3. The follower tries to mimic the dribbling maneuvers of the leader.

4. After 60 seconds partners switch roles and repeat.

5. Perform five or more 60-second rounds.

COACHING TIPS

-   Players should incorporate a variety of dribbling maneuvers as they move throughout the area.

SLALOM DRIBBLE

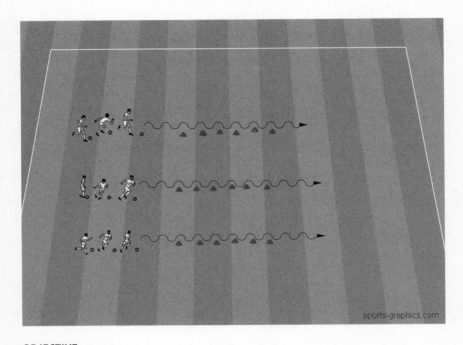

OBJECTIVE

*   To quickly change direction and/or speed while dribbling for close control

SETUP

*   Divide the team into groups of three to five players.

*   Position a line of six to eight markers in front of each group with distance of one yard between markers.

*   A ball is required for each player.

PROCEDURE

1. The first player in each group weaves (dribbles) in and out of the slalom markers while also keeping the ball in close control and stops at the final marker.

2. When the first dribbler gets to the final marker of the slalom course, the second player in line does likewise.

3. After all players have dribbled through the slalom, they repeat the course in the opposite direction.

4. Perform six to eight repetitions of the slalom.

COACHING TIPS

*   Encourage players to keep the ball close to their feet as they move in and of the slalom course.

ACCELERATION DRIBBLE

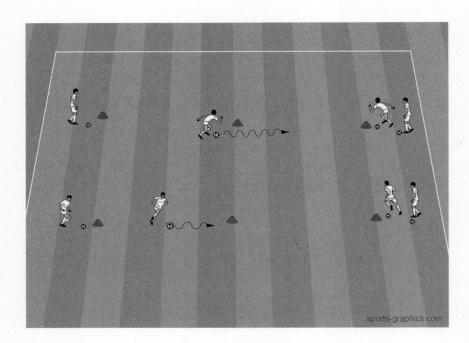

OBJECTIVE

- To improve player ability to take on and dribble past (bypass) an opponent

SETUP

- Form groups of four players.

- Place two markers about 25 yards apart for each group.

- Position an additional marker midway between the end markers to represent a stationary defender.

- Two players are positioned at each end marker and face the central marker.

- Each player has a soccer ball.

PROCEDURE

1. The first players (on both sides) alternately dribble at the central marker (imaginary defender).

2. As the dribbler approaches the central marker, he or she executes a sudden change of pace or acceleration to the right or left, pushing the ball past the imaginary defender, and then continues to dribble to the opposite line.

3. The next players in each line do likewise.

4. Continue the exercise for 10 minutes at a high level of speed.

COACHING TIPS

- Encourage the dribbler to make an explosive change of pace when pushing the ball past the central marker.

RACE THROUGH THE GATES

OBJECTIVE

- To improve dribbling skills

SETUP

- Play within an area of 30 yards square.

- Position cones or similar markers to represent five to eight mini-goals (gates) at various spots in the area.

- Each goal is about three yards wide.

- All players, each with a ball, are positioned within the area.

PROCEDURE

1. The players dribble among themselves within the area, keeping close control of the ball while avoiding contact with other players.

2. On the coach's verbal command "Change," all players execute a sudden change of pace and/or direction and dribble through the nearest small goal (gate) at top speed, after which they slow their dribble until the coach again issues the command "Change."

3. Coach issues the command every 15-20 seconds.

COACHING TIPS

• This exercise emphasizes essential elements of dribbling—the ability to change speed and direction quickly while keeping close control of the ball.

CREATIVE DRIBBLING

OBJECTIVE

• To improve dribbling ability in a restricted space

SETUP

• All players, each with a ball, take a position within an area of 30 yards square.

PROCEDURE

1. On the coach signal, all players dribble freely inside of the area while avoiding contact with any other players.

2. Players adjust their dribbling style as directed by the coach.

3. Coach commands may include, but are not limited to, the following:

    • Freeze! Players immediately stop the ball, then continue.

    • Dribble faster or slower.

    • Spin turn. (Player steps on ball to stop it, spins with ball 180 degrees in the opposite direction, and continues dribbling.)

    • Specific dribble moves (e.g., scissors, step over, lunge, cut in or out).

COACHING TIPS

• Encourage players to maintain close control of the ball at all times.

FIRST TO THE FLAG AND BACK

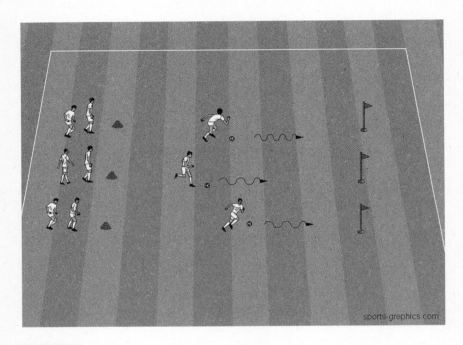

sports-graphics.com

OBJECTIVES

- To improve dribbling speed

- To provide fitness training

SETUP

- Organize teams of three or four players.

- Use the end line of the field as a start line.

- Teams are positioned side by side in single file behind the start line with 2 yards distance between teams.

- Place a flag or similar type marker 25 yards in front of each team.

- The first player in line for each team has a ball.

PROCEDURE

1. On the coach's command "Go," the first player in each line dribbles as fast as they can to the flag and back to the start line where he or she exchanges the ball with the next player in line.

2. All players in turn dribble to the flag and back to the start line as fast as possible.

3. The team completing the relay in the shortest time wins the race.

4. Repeat several times with a short rest between each race.

COACHING TIPS

- Explain to players that the technique used to dribble in open space differs from that used when dribbling for close control when in a crowd of players.

- Players should push the ball several steps ahead with the outside surface of the foot, sprint to catch up to it, and push it again.

DRIBBLE FOR POSSESSION, DRIBBLE FOR SPEED

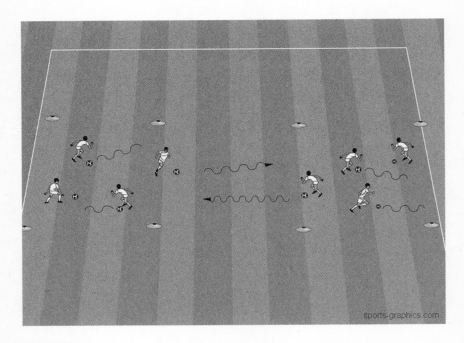

OBJECTIVE

- To practice various dribbling techniques

SETUP

- Divide the team into two groups.

- Position markers to outline two 15-yard squares, with 20 yards of distance between the squares.

- Station a group in each square

- A ball is required for each player.

PROCEDURE

1. On the coach command, players dribble within their square, using all surfaces of the foot to maintain close control of the ball.

2. Every few seconds the coach verbally signals players to quickly change direction and execute deceptive dribbling movements such as a stepover or scissors maneuver.

3. After 40–50 seconds of dribbling within their square the coach shouts "GO" which signals players to dribble at top speed from their square into the opposite square.

4. Upon entering the opposite square players slow their pace and continue to dribble among themselves until the coach again signals for them to return to their original grid. Repeat several times.

COACHING TIPS

• Reduce the size of the squares and increase the distance between squares for more advanced players.

BUMPER CARS

OBJECTIVE

- To incorporate changes of direction and speed into dribbling technique

SETUP

- Place markers to outline an area of 25-yards square.

- All players are stationed within the area, each with a ball.

PROCEDURE

1. All players begin dribbling randomly within the area while maintaining close control of their ball.

2. Players function as bumper cars: When a dribbler nears within 3 feet of another dribbler both players suddenly bounce (dribble) away from one another in different directions.

3. Continue nonstop for 10 minutes.

COACHING TIPS

• Encourage players to keep close control of their ball while making sudden changes of direction as they bounce away from other players.

CATCH ME IF YOU CAN

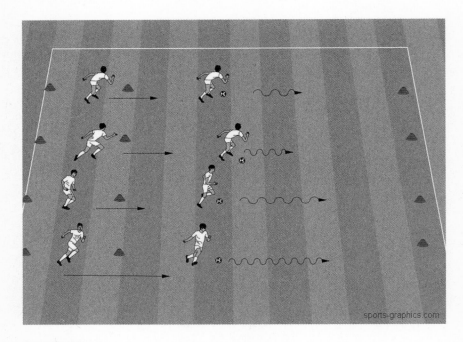

sports-graphics.com

OBJECTIVES

- To increase dribbling speed in open space

- To improve fitness

SETUP

- Each player partners with a teammate.

- Use the end line of the field as a starting line.

- One player (with a ball) is positioned 5 yards off the end line.

- His or her partner (without a ball) is positioned on the end line.

- Place a marker 20 yards from the end line directly in front of each pair of players.

PROCEDURE

1. On the coach command "GO," the player with the ball, who has a 5-yard head start, dribbles as quickly as possible to the marker and deposits the ball there.

2. The chasing player (without a ball) tries to arrive at the marker before the dribbling player.

3. The first partner to arrive at the marker wins the race.

4. Partners return to the starting line, switch roles, and repeat.

5. The first partner to win five races wins the competition.

COACHING TIPS

•   Adjust the distance covered to match the age and fitness level of players.

EVADE THE TACKLE

OBJECTIVE

- To incorporate dribbling and tackling skills in the same activity

SETUP

- Position markers to outline an area 20 yards wide by 35 yards long with a safety zone 5 yards deep at each end.

- Station three defenders in the center of the field.

- All remaining players, each with a ball, are positioned in a safety zone facing the defenders.

PROCEDURE

1. On the coach command, the players in the safety zone attempt to dribble the length of the channel into the opposite safety zone.

2. Defenders can eliminate dribblers by tackling their ball and kicking it out of the field area.

3. Dribblers who lose possession of their ball become defenders for the next round.

4. Dribblers who reach the safety zone with possession of their ball remain there until the coach issues the command to return to the original safety zone.

5. Players dribble back and forth between safety zones until all but three have been eliminated.

6. These players are the initial defenders for the next game.

COACHING TIPS

- Adjust the area to match the ages, abilities, and number of players involved.

- Prohibit slide tackles—block and poke tackles only!

1-VS-1 POSSESSION

OBJECTIVES

- To receive and maintain possession of the ball when under challenge from an opponent

- To practice shielding, dribbling, and tackling skills

SETUP

- Position markers to outline a 15-yard square area.

- Pair players for 1 vs 1 competition.

- Coach stations outside of the area with a supply of balls.

PROCEDURE

1. Two players enter the grid for 1-vs-1 competition.

2. Designate one player as the attacker and the other as the defender.

3. Coach initiates action by passing a ball to the attacker.

4. The defender attempts to gain possession of the ball; the attacker tries to maintain possession.

5. The attacker scores one point if he or she can maintain possession of the ball for 10 seconds and then return (pass) the ball to the coach (server).

6. The defender scores one point if he or she wins the ball before the attacker can return the ball to the coach.

7. Play 8 to 10 rounds with players alternating as attacker and defender with each round.

COACHING TIPS

- Encourage the attacker to use sudden changes of speed and direction to separate from the defending player.

DRIBBLE OR DEFEND

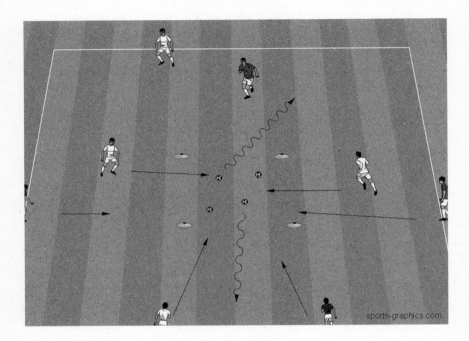

OBJECTIVES

- To improve dribbling speed and effectiveness

- To practice defending in a 1-vs-1 situation

- To improve fitness

SETUP

- Use markers to outline an area of 30 yards square.

- Outline a 10-yard square in the center of the larger area.

- Split the group into two teams of four to six players each.

- Players from both teams, without soccer balls, are positioned along the perimeter lines of the larger square

- Place a supply of balls (one-half as many as the number of players involved) in the smaller central square.

- Use colored vests to differentiate teams.

PROCEDURE

1. On the coach's command "Go!," players sprint to the central square and compete for possession of a ball.

2. Those who secure a ball attempt to dribble out of the larger square.

3. Players who do not immediately secure a ball must chase those who have a ball to prevent them from dribbling out of the larger square.

4. If a player steals a ball, the roles immediately reverse; he or she attempts to dribble out of the large square and the player who lost possession defends.

5. The round ends when all balls have been deposited outside of the large square.

6. The team that dribbles the most balls out of the large square is awarded one point.

7. Play ten rounds. The team scoring the most points after ten rounds wins the competition.

COACHING TIPS

- Prohibit slide tackles, particularly those initiated from behind.

HUNTED VS HUNTERS

OBJECTIVE

- To improve dribbling and shielding skills

SETUP

- Form groups of three players.

- Use markers to outline a 15-by-15-yard area for each group.

- All three players, each with a ball, position themselves along the perimeter of the area.

- Designate one player as the hunted and the other two as hunters.

PROCEDURE

1. On coach command, the player who is hunted dribbles into the area.

2. The hunters immediately follow (dribble after) and attempt to pass and contact the hunted player's ball with their own.

3. The hunted player attempts to protect their ball from the hunters by making sudden changes of speed and direction while shielding and maintaining close control of the ball.

4. The hunted player is penalized one point for each time his or her ball is contacted by a ball passed by the hunters.

5. Play for 60 seconds, after which players switch roles and repeat the drill.

6. Continue until each player has taken two turns as the hunted player.

7. The player with the fewest penalty points wins the game.

COACHING TIPS

- Make the drill more challenging by adding an additional hunter to the game or reducing the size of the playing area.

ONE VS ONE TO THE END LINE

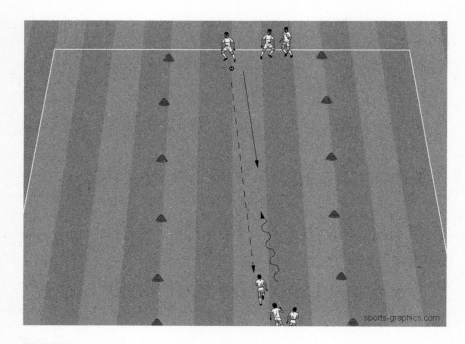

OBJECTIVE

• To improve player ability to take on and beat (bypass) an opponent on the dribble

SETUP

• Split the group into two teams of equal numbers.

• Position markers to create a 20-yard long by 15-yard wide channel.

• Each player partners with an opponent for 1-vs-1 competition.

• One ball is required for each pair.

• Partners position themselves on opposite end lines of the channel.

PROCEDURE

1. The partner with the ball passes to the opponent positioned on the opposite end line and immediately moves forward as the defender in 1-vs-1 situation.

2. The player receiving the ball attempts to dribble past their opponent and across the opposite end line with control of the ball.

3. The dribbler must stay within the side boundaries of the channel.

4. After a score, change of possession, or when the ball travels out of the field area, both players return to their respective end lines and the next pair compete 1-vs-1.

5. Partners alternate playing as the defender and attacker (dribbler) in each round.

COACHING TIPS

*   Encourage the dribbler to attack at speed and use deceptive movements to unbalance the defender.

ONE VS TWO TO THE END LINE

OBJECTIVE

- To develop teamwork between the (first) pressuring defender and (second) covering defender

SETUP

- Use markers to outline a 20-yard long by 15-yard wide channel.

- Divide the team into two groups: defenders and attackers.

- Defenders wear a distinctive colored vest and are positioned at one end of the channel.

- Attackers are positioned on the opposite end line from the defenders.

- Coach (server) is positioned to the side of the channel with a supply of balls.

PROCEDURE

1. Coach passes a ball to an attacker who immediately dribbles forward.

2. Two defenders advance off the opposite end line to confront the dribbler.

3. The first defender applies pressure on the ball and the second defender provides cover (protects the space behind) for the first defender.

4. The drill ends when the defenders win the ball or the attacker dribbles over the defenders' end line (must do so within the width of the channel).

5. Coach immediately then serves a ball to the next attacker and pair of defenders and play continues.

6. Repeat rounds so that each player takes a few repetitions as each (first and second) defender; groups then switch roles and repeat.

COACHING TIPS

*   The first defender (nearest defender to the ball) should apply immediate pressure to delay the attacker's (dribbler) forward progress.

*   The second (covering) defender protects the space behind the first defender in the event the first defender is beaten on the dribble.

DRIBBLE THROUGH THE CENTRAL GOAL

sports-graphics.com

OBJECTIVES

• To improve dribbling and passing skills

• To practice small group attacking and defending combinations

SETUP

• Position markers to outline a 25-yard square area.

• Position two additional markers in the center of the area to represent a 4-yard-wide goal.

• Form two teams of three players each; use colored vests to differentiate teams.

- Designate two additional players as neutrals who always play with the team in possession of the ball to create a 5-vs-3 player advantage for the team in possession.

- Teams and neutral players wear different colored vests.

- Award one team possession of the ball to begin.

PROCEDURE

1. Begin with a kickoff with the ball spotted along a perimeter line of the area.

2. Teams score a point by dribbling through either side of the central goal.

3. All players, including the neutrals, are allowed to score goals.

4. Change of possession occurs after a goal is scored, when the ball travels out of the field area, or when a defending player steals the ball. Otherwise, play is continuous.

5. A ball played out-of-bounds is returned by a throw-in.

6. Regular soccer rules are in effect except that the offside rule is waived.

COACHING TIPS

- Place restrictions on more experienced players (such as only two- or three-touch passes permitted).

KNOCKOUT

OBJECTIVE

* To improve dribbling, shielding, and tackling skills

SETUP

* Position markers to outline an area 30 yards square.

* All players but two are positioned within the area, each with a ball.

* Those two players (defenders) without a ball position themselves outside of the area and wear a distinctive colored vest.

PROCEDURE

1. All players positioned within the area begin dribbling among themselves, keeping close control of their ball while practicing sudden changes of speed, direction, and deceptive movements.

2. On the coach command the two players without a ball enter the area and attempt to dispossess dribblers of their ball and then kick it out of the field area

3. A dribbler whose ball is kicked out of the area immediately retrieves it and re-enters the exercise.

4. Play for 120 seconds at maximum effort, then select two new defenders and repeat.

5. Continue the exercise until all players have taken a turn as defenders.

COACHING TIPS

*   Encourage dribblers to use changes of direction and pace to elude the defenders and maintain possession of their ball.

JAIL BREAKOUT

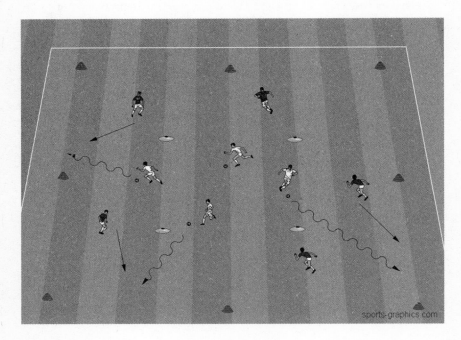

OBJECTIVE

- To practice dribbling and tackling skills in the same activity

SETUP

- Position markers to outline a 40-yard square area.

- Place four additional markers to outline a 15-by-15-yard square in the center of the larger square.

- Divide the group into two teams of four to eight players each.

- Station one team within the smaller square, each player with a ball.

- The opposing team's players, without balls, position themselves within the larger square but outside of the small central square.

- Teams wear different colored vests.

PROCEDURE

1. Players within the smaller square dribble among themselves, keeping close control of their ball.

2. Players on the opposing team, without soccer balls, jog slowly in the area outside of the smaller square but within the larger square.

3. On the coach's command players exit the small square and attempt to dribble out of the larger square.

4. Opposing team players act as defenders and try to prevent the dribblers from exiting the larger square by tackling their ball and kicking it away.

5. A player who successfully dribbles out of the larger square with control of the ball is awarded one point.

6. The dribbling team totals their points scored for the round.

7. Teams then switch roles and repeat for the next round of play.

8. Play a total of four rounds (two rounds for each team as dribblers).

9. Team scoring the most total points after four rounds wins the competition.

COACHING TIPS

- Prohibit the use of slide tackles to win the ball.

FIRST TO THE PENALTY AREA

OBJECTIVE

*   To improve dribbling speed; to practice recovery runs and tackling skills

SETUP

*   Play on a full-size regulation field with marked penalty areas.

*   Organize two teams of four to six players each.

*   Give each team a country name, for example, France and Germany.

*   Players from both teams, each with a ball, are stationed within the center circle of the field.

*   Designate each team to defend a penalty area of the field.

*   Use colored vests to differentiate teams.

*   No goals or goalkeepers are required.

PROCEDURE

1. Players from both teams dribble randomly among themselves within the center circle, avoiding contact with any other player.

2. After 20 to 30 seconds of continuous dribbling the coach shouts out a team name, for example "Germany!"

3. All players on team Germany immediately exit the center circle to dribble at top speed toward their opponent's penalty areas.

4. Players on the France team leave their balls in the center circle and give chase, attempting to catch and dispossess German players of their ball before they can dribble into France's penalty area.

5. A France player who tackles and wins a ball from a German player attempts to return it into the center circle by dribbling. The player who lost possession tries to prevent their opponent from deposing the ball in the center circle.

6. Play ten rounds with teams alternating from attack (dribbling) to defense with each round.

7. The dribbling team is awarded one point for each ball dribbled into the opponent's penalty areas.

8. The defending team is awarded two points for each ball stolen and returned to the center circle.

9. The round ends when all balls have been dribbled into the penalty area or returned into the center circle.

10. The team scoring the most points wins the competition.

COACHING TIPS

- Adjust the field size to accommodate the age and abilities of the players.

DRIBBLE THE OPEN GOAL

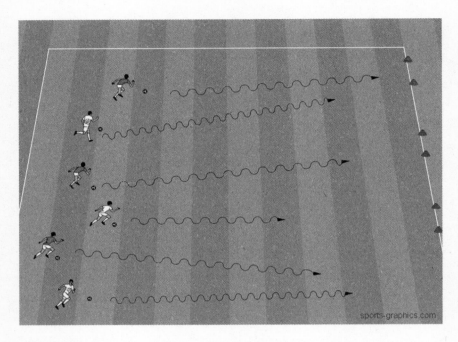

OBJECTIVE

- To improve dribbling speed in a competitive setting

SETUP

- Position markers to outline a 30-yard square area.

- Form teams of three players each.

- Position additional markers to represent four small goals, each two yards wide, spread out evenly on one side of the area.

- Two teams, each player with a ball, position themselves on the opposite side of the area from the goals.

PROCEDURE

1. On the coach's command all six players attempt to dribble as fast as possible through one of the four small goals on the opposite side of the area.

2. When a player dribbles through a goal, that goal becomes closed to other dribblers.

3. Award one team a point for each dribbler who is the first through an open goal.

4. The team scoring most points wins the round.

5. Teams return to the goal line and repeat the round.

6. Play a total of ten rounds.

7. The team totaling the most points after ten rounds wins the competition.

COACHING TIPS

• Require dribblers to step on the ball and stop it within two yards of the goal after dribbling through it.

DRIBBLE IN, DRIBBLE OUT, PASS IT ON

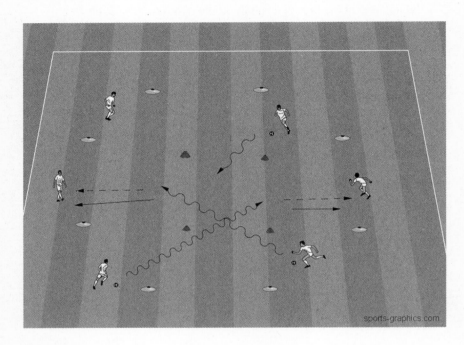

sports-graphics.com

OBJECTIVE

- To practice dribbling and passing skills in the same exercise

SETUP

- Play within a large circle outlined with markers.

- Position four additional markers to form a 5-yard square in the center of the circle.

- Six to eight players, evenly spaced apart, are positioned on the perimeter of the circle.

- Half of those players have a soccer ball; the others do not.

PROCEDURE

1. On the coach's signal the players on the perimeter who have a ball dribble at top speed into the central square, immediately exit the square from a different side than they entered, and then pass their ball to a player on the perimeter.

2. The passer immediately exchanges places with the player on the perimeter that they passed the ball to.

3. The player receiving the pass repeats the sequence of dribble into the square, dribble out of the square, and pass to a perimeter player.

4. Continue at maximum speed for ten minutes.

COACHING TIPS

•   Emphasize the importance of close control of the ball when entering and exiting the central square.

LATERAL SPEED DRILL

OBJECTIVES

- To practice deceptive foot movements and body feints used to unbalance an opponent

- To practice sudden changes of speed and direction while maintaining close control of the ball

SETUP

- Each player pairs up with a teammate for competition.

- Position two markers 10 yards apart for each pair of players.

- Players are positioned on opposite sides of the markers facing one another.

- One player has the ball.

PROCEDURE

1. The player with the ball attempts to dribble laterally to either marker before their partner can position his or her foot there.

2. Neither player may cross the imaginary line that separates them.

3. Play continuously for 60 seconds.

4. After a short rest, players exchange possession of the ball and repeat.

5. Play four rounds; each player plays two rounds as the attacker (dribbler) and two rounds as the defender.

6. The dribbler scores one point for each time he or she arrives at a side marker with the ball before the defender can position there.

7. The player who scores the most points wins the competition.

COACHING TIPS

- Encourage the attacker to use deceptive body movements coupled with sudden changes of speed and direction to unbalance the defender.

- Defenders should always maintain balance and body control.

DRIBBLE FOR CONTROL, DRIBBLE FOR SPEED

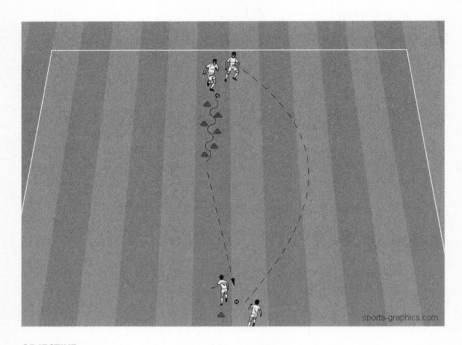

OBJECTIVE

- To improve dribbling skills for both speed and close control

SETUP

- Organize groups of four to six players.

- Place six to eight markers in a line to create a slalom course for each group, with one yard between markers.

- All players but one, each with a ball, are positioned in a single file line at the first marker.

- The one player without a ball is positioned 10 yards beyond the final marker, facing their teammates.

PROCEDURE

1. The first player in line dribbles through the slalom course of markers, keeping close control of the ball.

2. When reaching the last marker, the dribbler passes to the teammate 10 yards beyond that marker and takes their position.

3. The player receiving the ball dribbles at top speed directly back to the first marker and takes a position at the end of the line of players there.

4. The second player in line begins to dribble the slalom when the first player is about halfway through the course.

5. Continue until each player has completed at least 10 repetitions thru the slalom and back to the start position.

COACHING TIPS

*   When dribbling through the slalom course players should keep the ball close to their feet as they move in and out of the markers.

*   When dribbling for speed players should push the ball a couple of feet ahead, sprint to the ball, and push it again.

SECTION 3
PASSING AND RECEIVING

"Eleven individuals playing as one" is a common adage in the sport of soccer. Passing and receiving skills provide the vital thread needed to accomplish that objective—to connect and organize the individual parts of the team, the players, into a smoothly functioning whole. The ability of players to pass the ball accurately and with proper pace is necessary for the team to maintain possession of the ball and create successful attacking combinations. Equally important is the ability to skillfully receive and control balls arriving on the ground and through the air. All field players, as well as the goalkeeper, should become confident and competent in passing and receiving skills.

In most situations the ball should be passed along the ground rather than through the air. Ground passes are easier to receive and control and can be played with greater accuracy than passes lofted through the air. There will be times during a match, however, when the situation dictates the ball be passed through the air. For example, an opponent may be blocking the passing lane between the player with the ball and a teammate stationed in a dangerous attacking position, or the player with the ball might decide to quickly change the point of attack by flighting a long diagonal pass into the space behind the opposing team's backline.

Rolling (ground) balls are generally received with either the inside or outside surface of the foot, although the sole of the foot can also be used to control an oncoming ball. Balls taken directly out of the air can be received with the instep, thigh, chest, or, in rare instances, the head. In all cases, the player should withdraw the receiving surface as the ball arrives to cushion the impact and provide a soft target.

A player's initial touch as he or she receives the ball is their most important touch. Players who can recognize pressure and receive the ball into the space away from a challenging opponent will provide themselves additional time and space in which to initiate their next movement. Proper positioning of the body as the ball arrives is also important for maintaining possession, particularly when an opponent is challenging to win the ball. These points should be emphasized in all passing and receiving exercises.

The drills described in this section focus on the development of fundamental passing and receiving skills, although other skills are involved as well. The overriding objective of each drill is for players to become more competent in successfully executing passing and receiving skills in game-like situations. The drills can be modified to accommodate the age, ability, and physical maturity of the participating players.

TWO TOUCH THROUGH THE CHANNEL

sports-graphics.com

OBJECTIVE

- To improve inside-of-the-foot passing technique

SETUP

- Each player pairs with a partner.

- One ball is required for every pair.

- Partners face one another at distance of eight to ten yards.

- Place two markers to represent a 4-yard-wide gate midway between partners.

PROCEDURE

1. While jogging in place partners pass a ball back and forth through the gate as quickly as possible without error using two touches to receive and return the ball.

2. Perform at maximum speed for 60 seconds, rest, and repeat.

COACHING TIPS

- As players improve their passing technique they can progress to one-touch passing back and forth through the gate.

- To perform the inside-of-the foot pass a player should turn the passing foot sideways, keep it firm, and contact the ball with the inside surface of the foot.

PASS TO THE OPEN TEAMMATE

OBJECTIVE

- To play quick, accurate inside-of-the-foot passes while maintaining proper body shape and balance

SETUP

- Organize groups of four players.

- For each group three players (servers 1, 2, and 3) are positioned side-by-side with two yards of distance between them.

- The fourth player (target) faces the servers at five yards of distance.

- Servers 1 and 2 each have a ball; server 3 does not have a ball to begin.

PROCEDURE

1. Server 1 begins the drill by passing the ball to the target who returns the ball using a one-touch inside-of-the-foot pass to the teammate who does not have a ball (server 3)

2. Server 2 immediately plays a ball to the target player, who returns it to the server (1) who is without a ball.

3. Continue at maximum speed for two minutes, after which one of the servers switches positions with the target and repeats the drill.

4. Repeat until each player has taken two turns as the target player.

COACHING TIPS

- Passes should be accurate and properly weighted.

- If a ball goes astray the drill continues with the second ball; there are no stoppages in play.

- All passes should be played on the ground.

PREPARE, PASS, AND FOLLOW THE PASS

OBJECTIVES

- To develop inside-of-the-foot passing technique

- To receive and pass the ball using only two touches

SETUP

- Organize groups of two or three players.

- Each group faces an opposing group at 10 to 12 yards of distance.

- The first player in one of the groups has the ball.

PROCEDURE

1. The player with the ball passes to the first player in the opposite line using the inside-of-the-foot pass technique and immediately follows the pass to the end of that line.

2. The player receiving the ball prepares it with the first touch, passes to the next player in the opposite line with the second touch, and quickly follows the pass to the end of that line.

3. Continue at a rapid pace for ten minutes so each player makes numerous passes and runs to the opposite group.

COACHING TIPS

*   Emphasize the importance of the first touch preparing the ball for the second touch.

PASS, SPIN, DO IT AGAIN

sports-graphics.com

OBJECTIVE

- To emphasize the importance of moving (checking) toward the ball when receiving a pass

SETUP

- Organize groups of three players each.

- Two soccer balls are required for each group.

- Position four markers in a straight line.

- The two middle markers should be four yards apart.

- The two outside markers should be three to four yards away from the nearest middle markers.

- Position a player (server), each with a ball, at each of the outside markers.

- The third player in the group (without a ball) takes position between the two middle markers.

PROCEDURE

1. Central player moves (checks) toward one of the servers.

2. The server on that side passes the ball to the checking player who returns the ball to server with the first touch using inside-of-foot pass technique.

3. The central player immediately spins and moves (checks) toward the opposite server to return the ball with the first touch.

4. Continue for 45–60 seconds at maximum speed.

5. Players then switch positions and repeat the process.

6. Continue until each player has taken three turns as the central (checking) player.

COACHING TIPS

- Passes should be played along the ground.

- As players become more confident make it a contest (e.g., how many passes can a player return to servers in 45 seconds without error?).

CONNECT THE DOTS

OBJECTIVE

• To pass and receive balls while in constant motion

SETUP

• Divide the group into two teams of five to seven players each.

• Outline a playing area 30-yards square.

• Label each player (in each group) with a number, beginning with 1 and continuing up through the number of players in the group.

• Two players in each group, for example 1 and 4, each have possession of a ball.

PROCEDURE

1. On coach command all players begin moving throughout the area.

2. Those players with a ball dribble while those without a ball move into positions to receive a pass from the player in their group numbered directly below them.

3. For example, player 1 always passes to player 2, player 4 always passes to player 5, 6 to 7, etc.

4. The highest numbered player in the group passes to player 1 to complete the passing circuit.

COACHING TIPS

• Encourage players to call for (demand) the ball when they move into position to receive a pass.

PASS AND MOVE TO OPEN SPACE

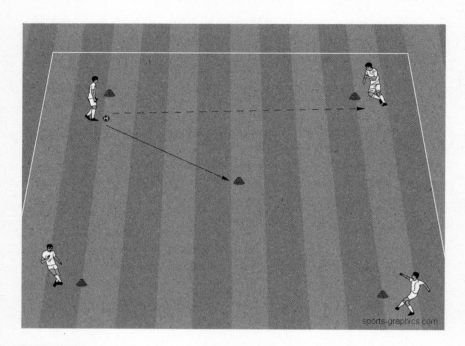

OBJECTIVE

- To develop the habit of passing the ball and immediately moving to open space for a possible return pass

SETUP

- Organize groups of four players each.

- Position four markers to represent the corners of a 20-yard square for each group.

- Place one additional marker near to the center of the square.

- Station a player at each corner marker to begin.

- One player in the group has the ball.

PROCEDURE

1. The player with the ball initiates play by passing the ball to one of the other players in the group and then immediately sprints to the open marker (marker without a player near it).

2. The player who receives the ball prepares to pass it with his or her first touch, passes the ball to another player with the second touch, and then sprints to the open marker.

3. Continues at a rapid pace as players receive, pass, and move to the open marker.

COACHING TIPS

*   Emphasize the concept of moving into open space after passing the ball.

*   Players should receive and prepare the ball with the first touch, then release the pass as quickly as possible with the second touch before sprinting to the open marker.

DIAMOND PASSING AND RECEIVING CIRCUIT

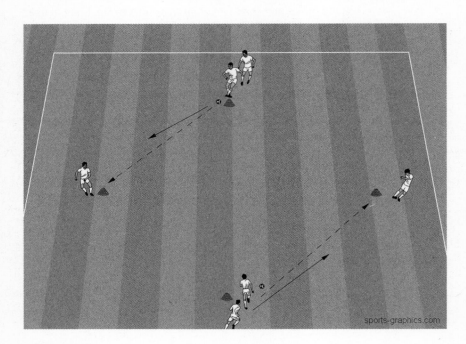

OBJECTIVES

- To receive, control, turn, and pass the ball using only two touches

- To practice making diagonal passes, the preferred type of pass in a match situation

SETUP

- Position four markers in the shape of a diamond approximately 15 yards wide and 15 to 18 yards deep.

- Position one player (without a ball) at each of the side markers.

- Position three or four players both the top and bottom of the diamond.

- One player at the top and one at the bottom of the diamond each have possession of a ball.

PROCEDURE

1. The player with the ball at both the top and bottom of the diamond pass to the teammate at the next marker (to the right), and immediately follow the pass to that spot.

2. The player receiving the ball positions sideways-on to the passer, turns with the ball as he/she receives it, passes to the player at the next marker, and follows the ball to that spot.

3. Players receive, pass, and follow their pass to the next marker in the diamond as quickly as possible.

4. Continue until each player has made 30 or more passes.

COACHING TIPS

-   The receiving player, who is positioned sideways-on to the passer, should receive the ball with the back foot and turn with the first touch, then pass to the next player in the diamond with the second touch.

-   With more advanced players include two or three balls in the exercise so that they are constantly receiving, passing, and moving to the next marker.

PASS OFF THE DRIBBLE

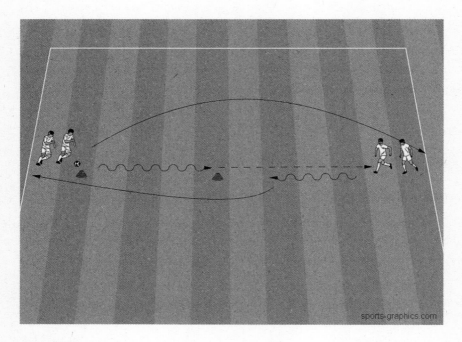

OBJECTIVE

- To perform dribbling and passing skills under the game-related pressure of player movement

SETUP

- Form groups of two or three players.

- Two groups face each other at 12 to 15 yards of distance.

- Place a marker midway between the two groups.

- The first player in one of the two groups has the ball to begin.

PROCEDURE

1. The player with the ball dribbles to the central marker, releases a pass to the first player in the opposite line, and then follows the ball to the end of that line.

2. The player who receives the ball does likewise in the opposite direction.

3. Continue at rapid pace as players pass off the dribble to a player in the opposite line.

COACHING TIPS

*   The ball should be passed firmly on the ground.

PASS IT ON, OR PASS IT BACK

sports-graphics.com

OBJECTIVE

- To encourage players to check (look) behind them for a challenging opponent while receiving a ball on the half turn

SETUP

- Use four markers to outline a 20-yard square area.

- Station two or three players at each corner of the area.

- A player in one corner of the area has a ball.

PROCEDURE

1. The drill starts as the player with the ball passes it to a player in an adjacent corner of the square and follows the pass to that corner.

2. As the ball arrives the receiving player checks over their shoulder to look for an imaginary defender challenging for the ball (the next player in line).

3. The next player in line holds up either one or two fingers.

4. The receiving player shouts out the number of fingers that the next player is holding up, receives the ball on the half turn, passes to the player at the next adjacent corner of the area, and follows the pass to that corner of the square.

5. Continue at rapid pace non-stop for 10 minutes.

COACHING TIPS

•   To make the game more realistic you can allow the visual cue to determine the receiving player's action as the ball arrives.

•   If the number called out is "One!" then the receiving player should turn with the ball and play/pass it on to the player at the adjacent corner,

•   If the number called is "Two!" then the receiving player should immediately pass the ball back to the player who passed him or her the ball.

PASS, RECEIVE, AND DRIBBLE HOME

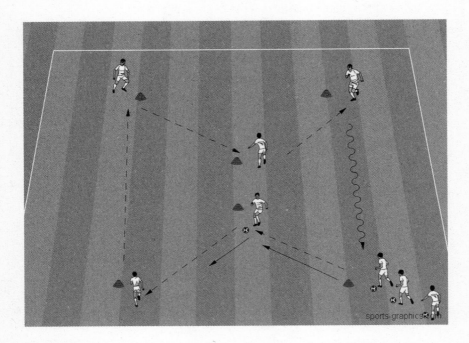

OBJECTIVE

- To receive and pass the ball accurately with limited touches

SETUP

- Play within a rectangular field area approximately 25 yards long and 15 yards wide.

- Place a marker (cone) at each corner of the area.

- Place two additional markers in the central area of the field.

- Station one player (without a ball) at each marker (except the marker at the lower right corner of the area).

- All remaining players, each with a ball, position at the lower right corner of the field area.

PROCEDURE

1. The first player at the lower right corner passes to the nearest central player and follows the pass to that spot.

2. The player receiving the ball turns and passes to the next player in the circuit and follows their pass to that position.

3. Continue the pattern of receiving the ball, immediately passing it on to the next player in the circuit, and then following the pass to that spot.

4. The player who receives the ball at the final marker (upper right corner of the field) dribbles at speed to the starting point (home).

5. Keep two or three balls in play to keep everyone constantly receiving, passing, and moving.

COACHING TIPS

*   Emphasize the importance of preparing to pass with the first touch on the ball.

TURN AND PLAY FORWARD

OBJECTIVE

- To receive and turn with the first touch on the ball

SETUP

- Form two groups of four to six players each.

- Groups, in single file lines, face one another at 15 yards of distance.

- The first player in one line has the ball.

PROCEDURE

1. The first player (with the ball) touches it a yard forward which is the signal for the first player in the opposite group to check (advance) toward the ball.

2. The player with the ball plays a firm pass on the ground to the advancing player who receives the ball and turns 180 degrees with the first touch.

3. The receiving player then passes to the next player in their line and follows the ball to the end of the line.

4. As the player receives the ball the next player in the opposite line checks toward the ball and repeats the process in the opposite direction.

5. Continue until each player has had 20 or more repetitions of receiving and turning with the first touch.

COACHING TIPS

*   Emphasize the importance of or receiving and turning with the ball in one fluid motion.

TURN AND PASS ON

OBJECTIVE

- To improve the technique used to receive and turn with the ball

SETUP

- Six to eight players position themselves on the perimeter of a large circle.

- Half of those players (servers) have a ball; half do not.

- Two or three players, without balls, are positioned within the circle.

PROCEDURE

1. On the coach command "Go!" the players stationed within the circle move (check) toward a perimeter player who has a ball to receive a pass from that player.

2. The player receiving the ball turns with their first touch, then passes it to a different player on the perimeter of the circle who is without a ball.

3. After passing the ball the player immediately advances toward a different perimeter player to receive a passed ball.

4. Central players receive, turn, and pass to a different player on the perimeter for as many repetitions as possible in the time allotted.

5. After two minutes the perimeter players switch places with the central players.

6. The original middle players take a position on the perimeter as passers.

7. Play several two-minute rounds, with a different group in the circle for each round.

COACHING TIPS

• Encourage players to receive and turn in one fluid motion.

RECEIVING AND CONTROLLING AIR BALLS

OBJECTIVES

- To receive and control balls directly out of the air

- To rehearse proper support positioning and movement for the teammate with the ball

SETUP

- Place markers to outline a playing area 30 by 25 yards.

- Organize two teams of four players each.

- Use colored scrimmage vests to differentiate teams.

- Award one team the ball to begin.

PROCEDURE

1. The team with possession of the ball attempts to play keep-away from their opponents.

2. Passing among teammates is accomplished by throwing, rather than kicking the ball.

3. Players must receive a ball tossed by a teammate with their instep, thigh, chest, or head, and then secure it with their hands before it drops to the ground.

4. Players may take up to five steps while in possession of the ball before passing to a teammate.

5. The defending team gains possession of the ball by intercepting an opponent's pass, or when an opponent fails to control the ball before it drops to the ground.

6. Players are not permitted to wrestle the ball away from opponents.

7. Award one team point for six or more consecutive passes without possession loss.

8. Play for 10 to 15 minutes.

9. The team scoring the most points wins.

COACHING TIPS

- Encourage players to withdraw the receiving surface (foot, thigh, etc.) as the ball arrives, to cushion the impact.

- Adjust the size of the area to accommodate the age and ability of players.

- This drill may not be appropriate for young players who have not mastered fundamental receiving skills.

SHORT – SHORT – LONG

OBJECTIVE

• To develop short-, medium-, and long-range passing skills

SETUP

• Organize groups of five or six players with one ball per group.

• Play on one half of a regulation field.

PROCEDURE

1. Players circulate (pass) the ball among their teammates while moving throughout the large field area.

2. Players must circulate passes among their teammates in a short-short-long passing sequence (i.e., two consecutive short distance passes [5 to 10 yards] followed by a longer pass [20 to 30 yards]) designed to change the point of attack.

3. The long pass is followed by another short-short-long sequence.

4. Short-range passes should be played on the ground; the longer-range passes can be played on the ground or lofted through the air.

COACHING TIPS

*   Emphasize accuracy and proper pace of passes.

*   Perform the drill at a rapid pace.

PINBALL

OBJECTIVE

- To improve one-touch passing skills

SETUP

- Place markers to outline an area 15 yards square.

- Six players participate in the drill.

- One player takes a position within the square as the defender.

- The remaining five players are designated as attackers.

- One attacker is positioned within the square.

- The other four attackers are positioned along the perimeter lines of the area.

- One attacker has possession of a ball to begin.

PROCEDURE

1. Attackers attempt to keep the ball from the defender by passing among themselves.

2. Attackers positioned on the perimeter lines are permitted to move laterally along the lines but may not move inward within the square.

3. The attacker who is stationed within the square is free to move anywhere within the square area to be available for a pass from teammates.

4. Attackers are restricted to one-touch passes only, thus the name, "Pinball."

5. If the ball travels out of the square because of an errant pass, or if the defender intercepts a pass, then the attacker who made the error becomes the defender.

6. The original defender becomes an attacker, and the drill continues.

COACHING TIPS

*   To make the game more challenging position two defenders within the square.

*   With novice (less skilled) players, enlarge the square and permit two-touch passing.

THREE VS ONE WITH ROTATING DEFENDERS

OBJECTIVE

- To improve player ability to pass, receive, and make correct decisions under the challenge of opponents

SETUP

- Play within a 12-by-15-yard area (grid size can vary depending on age and ability of players).

- Designate three players as attackers who position themselves within the grid area.

- All remaining players (defenders), each with a ball, are positioned at a corner of the area.

PROCEDURE

1. The first defender passes a ball to one of the three attackers and immediately enters the area to regain possession of the ball.

2. The three attackers attempt to maintain possession of the ball from the defender within the grid by using dribbling and passing skills.

3. If the defender wins the ball, or the ball leaves the area, the round ends and the next defender immediately passes a new ball to one of the attackers and the round is repeated.

4. Continue at rapid pace for three to four minutes, then replace the original three attackers with three of the original defenders and repeat.

COACHING TIPS

- Continue until all players have taken a turn as attackers and defenders.

THE KILLER PASS

OBJECTIVES

- To use passing and dribbling skills to keep possession of the ball from opponents

- To split (complete a penetrating pass between) the defenders (i.e., the killer pass)

SETUP

- Place markers to create a 15-by-20-yard playing area.

- Four players are positioned within the area as attackers.

- The remaining players (defenders) pair with a partner and position just outside the field area with a supply of balls.

PROCEDURE

1. The first pair of defenders passes a ball to an attacker and immediately enters the area to regain possession.

2. The four attackers attempt to keep the ball from the two defending players within the area.

3. Award attackers one point for completing five or more consecutive passes without loss of possession.

4. Award the attackers two points for a completed pass that splits (goes between) the defenders.

5. The round ends when a defender wins the ball, or the ball goes out of the area.

6. A different pair of defenders immediately serve a new ball to the attackers and play continues.

7. Continue for five to six minutes at a rapid pace, then designate four different attackers and repeat.

COACHING TIPS

• Encourage attackers to pass the ball quickly to unbalance the defenders.

• Emphasize the primary objective of splitting the defenders with the killer pass.

• Place restrictions on experienced players such as two-touch passing only.

PERIMETER PASSING

sports-graphics.com

OBJECTIVE

- To maintain possession of the ball through two-touch or one-touch passing combinations

SETUP

- Place markers to outline a circle with a diameter of 20 to 25 yards.

- Position six to eight players spaced evenly apart on the perimeter of the circle.

- Station two players (defenders) inside the circle.

- One ball is required for the drill; place a few extra balls outside of the circle as needed.

- A perimeter player has possession of the ball to begin.

PROCEDURE

1. The player with the ball passes to a teammate on the perimeter of the circle to initiate play.

2. Perimeter players attempt to keep the ball from the two defenders through quick one- and two-touch passes among themselves.

3. Perimeter players are permitted to move laterally along the perimeter of the circle but may not move inside the circle to receive a passed ball.

4. This restriction requires perimeter players to make short as well as longer passes to teammates positioned on the perimeter of the circle.

5. The two defenders work together to gain possession of the ball.

6. When a defender wins the ball the perimeter player who lost possession becomes a defender, and the defender becomes a perimeter player. Play is continuous.

COACHING TIPS

- Place restrictions on more experienced players; for example, prohibit passing the ball to the players directly next to them on the perimeter of the circle.

FIVE VS TWO RONDO WITH ROTATING DEFENDERS

sports-graphics.com

OBJECTIVE

- To maintain possession of the ball from outnumbered opponents

SETUP

- Divide the team into two groups of five (or six) players.

- Designate one group as attackers and the other as defenders.

- The attackers position themselves within a 15-by-20-yard area.

- The defenders pair with a teammate and position themselves just outside one corner of the area with the supply of balls.

PROCEDURE

1. The first pair of defenders passes a ball to one of the attacking players positioned within the grid.

2. Those two defenders immediately enter the area and attempt to regain possession of the ball from the five attackers, creating a 5-vs-2 situation inside the grid.

3. Play continues until the defenders win the ball, or the ball is kicked out of the area.

4. At that point the next pair of defenders immediately pass a ball into the area and play resumes.

5. Play for five minutes after which groups switch roles (defenders become attackers and attackers become defenders) and repeat the drill.

COACHING TIPS

• Encourage attacking players to move the ball quickly and utilize the entire space to create passing options.

SIX VS TWO TRANSITION TO TWO VS SIX

OBJECTIVE

- To maintain possession of the ball from outnumbered opponents

SETUP

- Play on an area 30 yards long by 15 yards wide divided lengthwise by a midline.

- Form two teams of six players each.

- Teams position themselves in opposite halves of the field.

- The coach is positioned outside of the field with a supply of balls.

PROCEDURE

1. The coach passes a ball to one of the teams.

2. The opposing team sends two players into that half of the field to gain possession of the ball from the six opponents.

3. If the two defending players gain possession, they pass the ball to a teammate positioned in their team's half of the field and immediately join their teammates.

4. Two members of the team that lost possession immediately follow to regain possession of the ball. If the two defenders regain possession of the ball, they pass it to their teammates in the opposite half of the field and join them to create a 6-vs-2 situation in that half.

5. Teams continue to play 6 vs 2 in each half of the field by repeating this pattern with every change of possession.

COACHING TIPS

- Encourage an immediate transition from attack to defense upon loss of possession.

- To make the drill more challenging, impose a touch restriction (only two or three touches permitted) to receive and pass the ball.

FIND THE TEAM TARGET

sports-graphics.com

OBJECTIVES

- To develop passing combinations among teammates

- To complete passes to a designated target player under the pressure of challenging opponents

SETUP

- Position markers to outline a playing area of approximately 35 yards square.

- Divide the group into two teams.

- Designate one player on each team as the target who wears a distinctive vest to differentiate him or her from teammates.

- One ball is required; place an extra supply of balls just outside of the field area.

PROCEDURE

1. Award one team the ball to begin.

2. Teammates pass among themselves to create an opportunity for a player to complete a pass to the team's target player.

3. Opponents try to gain possession of the ball and at the same time deny passes to the opposing team's target.

4. Change of possession occurs when a player intercepts an opponent's pass or tackles the ball from an opponent.

5. Teams score one point each time they can complete a pass to their target player.

6. After a point scored the target passes the ball to a teammate and play continues.

7. There is no change of possession after a point is scored.

8. The team scoring the most points wins the game.

COACHING TIPS

- Encourage the target player to constantly move into positions where he or she is available to receive a pass.

- Teammates try to move the ball quickly to unbalance opponents and create passing lanes to the team target player.

THREE TEAMS, FOUR GOALS, FIVE NEUTRALS

OBJECTIVE

* To rehearse passing combinations and movement patterns used to maintain possession of the ball from outnumbered opponents

SETUP

* Position markers to outline a 35-yard square playing area.

* Place a small goal (three yards wide) at each corner of the square.

* Organize three teams of five players each.

* Teams wear different colored scrimmage vests.

* One ball is required; an extra supply of balls is placed outside of the playing area in the event the ball is kicked away.

* Award one team possession of the ball to begin.

PROCEDURE

1. Two teams of five players are stationed inside the field area along with one member from the third team who plays as a neutral player who joins whichever team has the ball to create a 6-vs-5 player advantage for the team in possession within the field area.

2. The remaining four players of the third team position themselves along the perimeter of the square, one player on each sideline, and also function as neutral players who join the team with possession of the ball.

3. The team in possession can pass the ball to the perimeter neutral players when attempting to keep possession.

4. The perimeter players are not permitted to enter the playing area, however, but can move sideways (laterally) along the perimeter lines of the area to receive passes.

5. The perimeter players are restricted to two touches to receive and return the ball to a player on the team with possession.

6. A team is awarded one point for each time it completes six or more passes without loss of possession, and two points for each time it passes or shoots a ball into one of the four small goals.

7. The first team to score 10 points wins the game.

8. The losing team becomes the neutral players for the next round.

COACHING TIPS

• Adjust the size of the area to match the age and abilities of players.

SECTION 4
SHOOTING/FINISHING

Scoring goals is arguably the most difficult challenge facing soccer players. This is particularly apparent at the highest levels of competition where team defense is extremely organized, and goalkeepers are of the highest quality. It is not surprising that the player who can regularly deposit the ball into the back of the opponent's net is a highly coveted commodity.

The great goal scorers possess a rare and special talent—the ability to consistently create and finish scoring opportunities that most others do not. They are obviously extremely valuable to the team as they can determine the outcome of a match with one special strike of the ball. The immense salaries of players like Harry Kane, England international who has won the Premier League Golden Boot (top goal scorer) three times; Lionel Messi, arguably one of the greatest players in the history of the game; and the young and rising star Erling Halland of Manchester City, who recently set a Premier League single-season scoring record, attest to that fact. While it may be true that not every player can develop into an elite goal scorer, it is a fact that every player can improve and sharpen their finishing skills. In doing so they will become a more complete player and assume a more expansive role in their team's attacking efforts.

To score goals on a regular basis is dependent upon several factors, one of which is the ability to strike the ball powerfully and accurately with either foot. Less tangible qualities such as anticipation, confidence, and composure under pressure also factor into the equation. Several different shooting techniques are used depending on whether the ball is rolling, bouncing, or contacted directly out of the air. The instep drive technique is most often used to strike a rolling or stationary ball. The full volley, half volley, and side volley techniques are used to strike a bouncing ball or a ball that is dropping from above.

The drills described in this section expose players to many of the competitive pressures they will face in actual game situations. Most drills can be easily modified to make them more or less difficult to successfully perform by adjusting variables such as the area size, the number of touches permitted to receive and shoot the ball, the number of repetitions, and the number of players involved.

TWO-TOUCH SHOOT TO SCORE

OBJECTIVE

- To improve player ability to receive, prepare, and shoot on goal using only two touches of the ball

SETUP

- Play at one end of a field with a full-sized goal.

- Coach (server) is positioned along the end line with a supply of balls.

- Players line up 25 yards front and center of goal.

- Goalkeeper is positioned in goal.

PROCEDURE

1. Server (coach) passes a ball from the end line toward the penalty spot.

2. The first player in line runs forward, prepares the ball with the first touch, and shoots to score with the second touch.

3. Player (shooter) retrieves the ball, deposits it with coach, and returns to the line of shooters.

4. Continue through the line as many times as desired.

COACHING TIPS

• Use two lines of players and two lines of servers, one on each side of the goal.

• As an alternative require players to shoot with the first touch.

PLAYING THE ANGLE

OBJECTIVES

- To receive, prepare, and shoot from various distances and angles in and around the penalty area

- To improve fitness

SETUP

- Play on one end of a regulation field with a penalty area and full-sized goal.

- Place five to six markers at various distances and angles in and around the penalty area.

- Goalkeeper is stationed in goal.

- Shooters position themselves on one side of the penalty area.
- Place a supply of balls and a server (passer) on the opposite side of the penalty area.

PROCEDURE

1. The first shooter sprints around the first marker, turns, and runs into the penalty area.

2. As the shooter enters the area the server passes a ball into the path of the shooter.

3. The shooter prepares the ball with the first touch, then shoots to score with the second touch.

4. The next shooter in line does likewise.

5. After taking the shot the player returns to the shooting line.

6. After all shooters have run around the first marker, they repeat around the second marker.

7. Continue until all shooters have taken shots from the various angles and distances to goal.

8. Repeat the shooting circuit several times with each player.

COACHING TIPS

- Emphasize the importance of preparing the ball with the first touch.
- Encourage players to perform the drill at game speed.

FOUR PASSES AND A SHOT

OBJECTIVES

- To develop shooting (finishing) skills

- To improve one-touch passing skills

SETUP

- Play on one end of a regulation field with a full-sized goal on the end line.

- Position a goalkeeper in goal.

- Each player pairs with a partner.

- One partner (shooter) is stationed with their back to the goal, 20 yards front and center of goal.

- The other partner (server), with a ball, is positioned 25 yards from goal facing his or her partner.

- Four additional soccer balls are placed close to the server.

PROCEDURE

1. Partners perform quick one-touch passes back and forth.

2. On the fourth pass the player (server) facing goal passes the ball past his or her partner (shooter) into the penalty area.

3. The shooter turns, sprints to the ball, and shoots at goal.

4. The shooter immediately returns to the original start position and repeats the pattern of four passes followed by a shot on goal.

5. Repeat for all five soccer balls (total of 20 one-touch passes between partners and five shots at goal).

6. Partners then switch roles and repeat for five soccer balls.

COACHING TIPS

- Passes should be firm and on the ground.

- The shooter should turn quickly, sprint to the ball, and then shoot to score.

QUICK ON THE TURN

OBJECTIVE

- To improve player ability to receive and turn with the ball in one fluid motion

SETUP

- Form groups of three or four players.

- Groups are stationed 25 yards from the goal in single file lines facing the goal with 5 yards distance between groups.

- Each player has a ball.

- Position markers to outline a 5-by-5-yard square 5 yards in front of each group.

- One player in the group (without a ball) is positioned in the square and faces the line of players.

PROCEDURE

1. The first player (server) in the line passes a ball to the player in the square.

2. The player receives and turns toward goal with the ball, pushes it forward (out of the square), and shoots to score.

3. Immediately after the shot the next group of players does likewise.

4. The player who passed the ball enters the square to be the next shooter.

5. The player who took the shot retrieves the ball and returns to the line of servers.

6. Continue until each player has taken several shots at goal.

COACHING TIPS

•   Emphasize proper instep drive shooting technique.

RAPID FIRE

OBJECTIVE

- To practice shooting skills under the game-related pressures of limited time, restricted space, and physical fatigue

SETUP

- Play on one end of a regulation field with a full-sized goal.

- The shooter is positioned at the top of the penalty area with their back to goal.

- The server (coach) is positioned 22–25 yards from goal facing the shooter, with a supply of six to eight balls.

- The goalkeeper is positioned in goal to save all shots.

PROCEDURE

1. The coach (server) passes a ball past the shooter (toward goal) who turns, sprints to the ball, and shoots at goal.

2. The shooter immediately sprints back to the start position.

3. The coach then plays another ball toward goal, this time to the opposite side of the shooter who shoots with the opposite foot.

4. Continue at rapid pace until the supply of balls is depleted.

COACHING TIPS

• Alternate shots with right and left feet.

• Reduce the shooting distance for younger players.

SCORE OFF THE SPEED DRIBBLE

OBJECTIVE

- To improve shooting technique when running with the ball at pace

SETUP

- Divide the team into three groups.

- Groups are positioned in single-file lines facing the goal at a distance of 25 yards with 8 to 10 yards between groups.

- Each player has a ball.

- Goalkeeper is positioned in goal.

PROCEDURE

1. The first player in each line alternately dribbles forward at speed, shoots to score from 15–18 yards of distance, retrieves the ball, and returns to the line of shooters.

2. After each shot the next player in line dribbles forward and does likewise.

3. Continue until each player has attempted several shots at goal.

4. To create competition between groups, award one point for a shot on goal and two points for a goal scored.

COACHING TIPS

•   Emphasize proper shooting technique (i.e., toe pointed downward, foot firm, ball contacted on instep).

SHOOT THEN SHOOT AGAIN

OBJECTIVES

- To sharpen shooting skills under the game-simulated pressure of physical fatigue

- To improve fitness

SETUP

- Play on one end of a regulation field with a full-sized goal on the end line.

- Position a goalkeeper in goal.

- Place four markers to form a 5-yard square at the top of the penalty arc, 22 yards from the goal.

- Deposit five or six soccer balls within the square.

- Position a player (shooter) on the penalty spot.

PROCEDURE

1. On the command "Go," the shooter sprints to the square, collects a ball, turns toward goal, dribbles forward a few steps, and shoots from distance of 15–18 yards.

2. The player immediately returns to the square, collects another ball, and repeats the sequence.

3. Continue at maximum effort until the supply of balls is exhausted.

COACHING TIPS

- Adjust the shooting distance to accommodate the age and ability of players.

- Encourage shooters to perform at game-like speed to simulate the pressures encountered in actual match situation.

- Players should alternate shooting with left and right feet.

DRIBBLE, PASS, SHOOT TO SCORE

OBJECTIVES

- To improve ability to shoot with power and accuracy off of a dribble/pass combination

- To provide goalkeeper training

SETUP

- Play on one end of a regulation field with a full-sized goal.

- Position markers 40 yards from the goal to represent the opposite end line of the field.

- Four or five players (shooters), each with a ball, are stationed at the end line of the field opposite the full-sized goal.

- A target player is positioned 15 yards from the goal, facing the shooters.

- Place five or six markers in a zigzag pattern to form a slalom course in front of the shooters.

- Goalkeeper is positioned in goal and attempts to save all shots.

PROCEDURE

1. Shooters, in turn, dribble at top speed through the slalom course while keeping close control of the ball.

2. Upon reaching the final marker the dribbler passes the ball to the target player positioned 15 yards front and center of the goal who lays the ball off to the side

3. The shooter sprints forward and strikes the ball with the first touch.

4. The shooter immediately retrieves the ball and returns to the start position.

5. The next shooter in line repeats the process.

6. Continue until each player has attempted ten or more shots at goal.

7. Award two points for a goal scored and one point for a shot on goal saved by the goalkeeper.

8. The shooter totaling the most points wins the competition.

COACHING TIPS

- Position the slalom course markers so that shooters are required to cut the ball sharply right and left when dribbling through them.

- Emphasize dribbling speed and close control.

TURN AND SHOOT TO SCORE

OBJECTIVE

- To turn the ball toward goal with the first touch, dribble, and release a shot on goal

SETUP

- Play on one end of a regulation field with full-sized goal on the end line.

- Place a marker 20 yards directly in front of the goal, to serve as an imaginary defender.

- Place another marker 30 yards in front and center of the goal.

- All players (servers) except one position themselves at that marker 30 yards from goal, each with a ball.

- One player (shooter) is positioned at the top of the penalty arc, with their back to goal and facing the line of servers.

PROCEDURE

1. First server in the line 30 yards from goal passes a ball along the ground to shooter.

2. The shooter moves toward the oncoming ball, receives and turns with the ball toward goal, dribbles at the imaginary defender, executes a dribbling maneuver to bypass the defender, and shoots at goal.

3. The shooter retrieves the ball and returns to the line of servers 30 yards from goal.

4. The player who passed the ball to the shooter moves to that spot to become the next shooter.

COACHING TIPS

- Place emphasis on a smooth turn toward goal with the first touch of the ball, then an explosive touch forward to beat the imaginary defender.

BOX TO BOX PRESSURE SHOOTING

sports-graphics.com

OBJECTIVES

- To develop power and shooting accuracy

- To improve fitness

- To provide goalkeeper training

SETUP

- Play on one end of a regulation field with a full-sized goal.

- Place markers to outline two 5-yard square boxes 18 yards from the goal, one on each side of the penalty arc.

- Place three or four soccer balls in each box.

- The shooter is positioned at the penalty spot facing the goal.

- A goalkeeper is positioned in goal.

PROCEDURE

1. On the coach command "Go," the shooter spins around, sprints to one of the boxes, collects a ball, dribbles into the penalty area, and shoots to score.

2. The shooter immediately turns, sprints to the opposite box, collects a ball, and repeats the sequence.

3. The shooter continues at maximum speed, alternating balls from one box to the other, until the supply of balls is exhausted.

4. Goalkeeper attempts to save all shots.

COACHING TIPS

- Require players to alternate shooting with right and left feet.

- Decrease or increase the number of shots depending upon age and fitness of the players involved.

TWO-TOUCH SHOOT TO SCORE

OBJECTIVE

• To prepare and strike the ball on goal using only two touches

SETUP

• Play on one end of the field with a full-sized goal and goalkeeper.

• Divide the team into groups of three or four players each.

• Position a group near to each goal post, each player with a ball.

• Position a group of players on each side of the half arc at the top of the penalty area (these players do not have a ball).

PROCEDURE

1. The first player positioned by the goal post plays a diagonal pass to a player positioned at the side of the half arc at the top of the penalty area.

2. The receiving player moves forward, prepares the ball with the first touch, and shoots on goal with the second touch.

3. After the shot at goal a player on the opposite side of goal plays a diagonal pass to a player on the opposite side of the half arc who advances to receive the ball, prepares it with the first touch, and shoots with the second touch.

4. Players follow their pass and/or shot to switch sides after each attempt.

COACHING TIPS

•   Emphasize the importance of the first touch setting up the shot.

RECEIVE, PREPARE, SCORE

OBJECTIVE

- To use only two touches to receive, prepare, and strike a ball on goal

SETUP

- Play on one end of a regulation field with a full-sized goal.

- Station a goalkeeper in goal who attempts to save all shots.

- Two lines of players position themselves facing one another along he top edge of the penalty area with 10–12 yards distance between lines.

- Each player in one of the lines (passing line) has a ball.

PROCEDURE

1. The first player in the passing line plays a ball to the first player in the shooting line who runs onto the ball, touches it toward goal with the first touch, and shoots to score with the second touch.

2. Both players follow up the shot to finish a potential rebounded save off the goalkeeper.

3. Both players (passer and shooter) then return to the opposite line from which they came and the next two players repeat the process.

4. Continue at rapid pace until each player has taken several shots on goal.

COACHING TIPS

- Emphasize the importance of the first touch preparing the second touch (shot at goal).

GOAL TO GOAL SHOOTING CIRCUIT

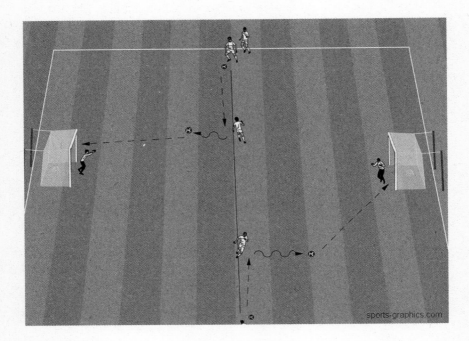

sports-graphics.com

OBJECTIVE

• To receive, prepare, and strike the ball on goal in one fluid movement

SETUP

• Use markers to outline a field 40 yards long and 40 yards wide, divided by a midline.

• Place a full-sized goal at the midpoint of each end line with a goalkeeper in each goal.

• Divide the team into two groups.

• Groups position themselves on opposite sides of the field at the midline.

• Each player has a ball.

PROCEDURE

1. One player (shooter) in each group moves on to the field (without a ball) along on the midline, about 10 yards in from the touchline.

2. The next player in line passes a ball to the shooter who turns the ball toward goal with the first touch, dribbles forward a couple of yards and then shoots to score.

3. The player who passed the ball to the shooter moves into position on the field to be the next shooter.

4. Groups on both sides shoot at the same time, but at opposite goals.

5. After shooting, the player retrieves the ball and joins the group on the opposite side of the field.

6. Continue at rapid pace until each player has taken numerous shots at goal.

COACHING TIPS

- Emphasize the importance of the first touch turning the ball toward goal in preparation for the shot.

GIVE AND GO WITH TARGET

OBJECTIVE

- To create and finish scoring opportunities off a give-and-go passing combination

SETUP

- Play on one end of a regulation field with full-sized goal.

- Players (shooters), each with a ball, line up 30 yards from goal.

- The target player is positioned 20 yards from the goal facing the shooters.

PROCEDURE

1. The first shooter in line dribbles forward, passes the ball to the target player, and sprints forward.

2. Target player lays the ball off a yard or so to either side.

3. The shooter strikes the ball first time at goal, retrieves the ball, and returns to the end of the shooting line.

4. Next player in line does likewise.

5. Repeat until each player has taken at least ten shots at goal.

COACHING TIPS

• Emphasize importance of a firm and accurate pass to the target player.

• Encourage players to perform at game speed.

DUMMY IT

OBJECTIVES

- To rehearse the movement patterns between two teammates

- To improve shooting ability

SETUP

- Play on one end of a regulation field with a full-sized goal.

- Position a goalkeeper in goal.

- Split the team into two groups (A and B).

- Group A players (servers/passers) position themselves in a single file line 35 yards from the end line, facing the goal. Each player has a ball.

- Group B players position themselves 15 yards from the end line, facing group A.

PROCEDURE

1. The first two players in group B sprint toward group A.

2. The second player follows the first player at 4 to 5 yards of distance.

3. The first player in group A passes a ball to the advancing group B players.

4. The first group B player steps over ("dummies") the ball and lets it roll to the trailing player.

5. The first group B player peels off to the side to receive a one-touch pass from the trailing teammate.

6. The first player prepares the ball toward goal with the first touch, then shoots with the second touch.

7. Both players return to their original line and the next three players repeat the dummy exercise.

8. Continue at rapid pace for 8 to 10 minutes after which the groups switch positions and repeat the exercise.

COACHING TIPS

*   The player who dummies the ball should perform a deceptive fake before peeling off to get a pass from the trailing player.

VOLLEY TO SCORE

OBJECTIVE

- To improve volley shotting technique

SETUP

- Play on one end of the field with a full-sized goal.

- Place a marker on the penalty spot.

- Player (shooter) is positioned at the marker.

- Coach (server) is positioned at one of the goal posts with a supply of balls.

- Do not use a goalkeeper (open goal).

PROCEDURE

1. Coach (server) tosses a ball that drops five to six yards directly in front of the goal.

2. The shooter moves forward and after the first bounce volleys the ball out of the air into the open goal.

3. The shooter immediately sprints back to the penalty spots, then repeats the drill.

4. Continue for six to eight consecutive volley shots, rest, then repeat.

COACHING TIPS

- Emphasize the correct volley technique—strike the ball on the laces of the shoe with the toes pointed downward and the foot firmly positioned.

- Player should alternate shots with left and right feet.

ATTACKER VS DEFENDER

OBJECTIVE

- To create competitive pressure in a 1-vs-1 situation to goal

SETUP

- Divide the team into two groups of equal numbers.

- Play on half of a regulation field (a third of a field for younger players) with a regulation goal centered on the end line (with goalkeeper).

- Teams position themselves on opposite sides of the center circle facing the goal.

- Each player pairs with a partner on the opposite team for a 1-vs-1 competition.

- Coach (server) is positioned in the center circle with a supply of balls.

PROCEDURE

1. Coach passes a ball directly toward the goal.

2. Partners immediately sprint forward to compete for possession of the ball.

3. The player gaining possession attempts to score; the partner defends.

4. Roles reverse upon change of possession.

5. Continue until a shot on goal is taken, the ball goes out of bounds, or a goal is scored.

COACHING POINTS

- The player gaining possession should drive straight to goal and use his or her body to shield/protect the ball from the trailing defender.

TURN, DRIBBLE, SHOOT TO SCORE

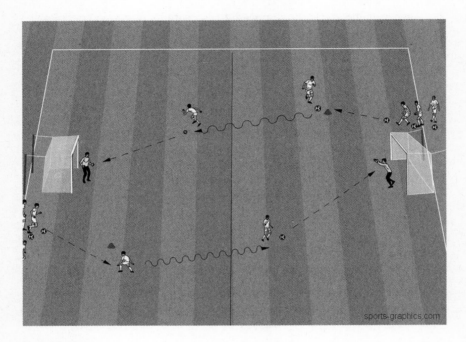

OBJECTIVE

- To improve ability to shoot with power and accuracy when dribbling at speed

SETUP

- Play on a 50-yard-long by 40-yard-wide field area, divided lengthwise by a midline.

- Center a regulation goal on each end line.

- Organize two groups of six to eight players each, plus goalkeepers.

- Groups position themselves on opposite end lines next to the goal diagonally across the field from one another.

- Position a marker 10 yards on to the field in front of each group.

- Position one player—the shooter—without a ball at the marker.

- All other players in the group, each with a ball, line up in single file facing the shooter.

PROCEDURE

1. The first player in line (for both groups) passes a ball to the player (shooter) positioned at the marker 10 yards onto the field.

2. As the shooter receives the ball he or she turns and dribbles at speed toward the opposite goal.

3. When the shooter crosses the midline, he or she releases a shot at goal.

4. The shooter retrieves the ball and joins the group at that end of the field to repeat the drill in the opposite direction.

5. The player who passed the ball takes up a position at the marker as the next shooter (without a ball) for the next repetition.

6. Continue at rapid pace until each player has taken at least ten shots at goal.

COACHING TIPS

- Encourage players to take a direct route toward the goal at top speed.

PLAY OFF THE WALL

OBJECTIVE

- To create scoring opportunities off of a wall pass combination with a teammate

SETUP

- Play on one end of a regulation field.

- Place four markers in the shape of a 5-yard square at the top of the penalty arc, front and center of the goal.

- Position a player (i.e., the wall) without a ball at each of the markers closest to the goal.

- All other players (shooters), each with a ball, are stationed at the markers farthest from the goal, facing the wall players.

PROCEDURE

1. The first shooter in one of the lines plays a firm pass to the wall player positioned diagonally ahead of him or her.

2. The wall player redirects the ball into the central area of the square.

3. The shooter advances, pushes the ball toward goal with the first touch, and shoots to score with the second touch.

4. The wall player retrieves the ball and moves to the shooting line.

5. The original shooter assumes the wall position for the next shooter.

6. Lines alternate turns with each shot on goal.

COACHING TIPS

•   Emphasize the importance of performing the drill at game-like speed.

TWO VS ONE ZONE TO ZONE

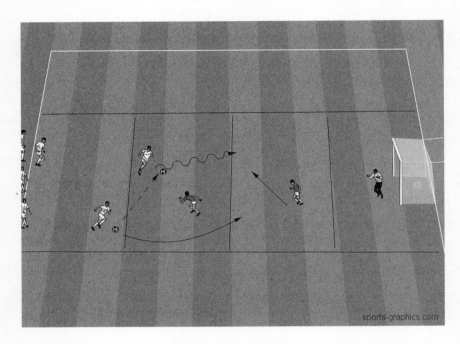

sports-graphics.com

OBJECTIVES

• To use the give-and-go pass to bypass an opponent in a 2-vs-1 situation

• To finish goal-scoring opportunities

SETUP

• Play on one end of a regulation field with a full-sized goal.

• Position markers to outline three consecutive 10-yard long and 20-yard-wide zones in front of the goal.

• Position a single defender in each of the two zones furthest from the goal (not the zone nearest to the goal).

• Goalkeeper is positioned in the goal.

- Organize teams of two players each.

- Teams position themselves at the end line opposite the goal.

- Each team has a ball.

PROCEDURE

1. The first team of two players dribbles into the first zone and attempts to beat/bypass the single defender in that zone to enter the second zone with possession of the ball.

2. If successful they then attempt to beat the defender in the second zone to enter the final (third) zone.

3. Once entering the third zone (nearest to the goal), the player with the ball takes a shot at goal.

4. The goalkeeper attempts to save all shots.

5. If a defender wins the ball in any zone, the round is over and the next team of two attackers enters the first zone to repeat the exercise.

6. After several rounds, rotate new defenders into the zones and repeat.

COACHING TIPS

- Encourage the player with the ball to dribble at (commit) the defender and then execute the give-and-go pass with teammate to bypass the defender and enter the next zone.

THROW, CATCH, AND VOLLEY TO SCORE

OBJECTIVE

• To score off volley shots with power and accuracy

SETUP

• Place markers to outline a rectangular playing area 30 yards by 25 yards.

• Position a full-sized goal at the center of each end line.

• Form teams of four (or five) field players plus a goalkeeper.

• Use colored vests to differentiate teams.

PROCEDURE

1. Two teams enter the field area to compete.

2. Award one team possession of the ball to begin.

3. Teammates pass the ball by throwing and catching with their hands rather than their feet.

4. Each team defends a goal and can score by striking a volley shot (directly out of the air) into the opponent's goal.

5. A player may take no more than five steps with the ball before releasing (passing) it to a teammate.

6. Change of possession occurs when an opposing player intercepts a pass, when the ball goes out of play last touched by an attacking player, when the ball is dropped to the ground, when a player takes more than five steps without passing the ball, or after a goal is scored. Otherwise, play is continuous.

7. The team scoring the most goals wins the game.

COACHING TIPS

- Encourage players to move into positions to be available for passes from teammates.

- Emphasize correct volley shot technique—toes pointed downward, foot firm, ball contacted on the instep.

- This drill may not be appropriate for young or inexperienced players.

SHOOT TO SCORE, THEN SET TO SAVE

OBJECTIVE

• To improve shooting/finishing skills

SETUP

• Play on one end of a regulation field with a full-sized goal on the end line.

• Divide the group into two teams.

• Team 1 players position themselves next to a goal post, while team 2 players position themselves at the opposite goal post.

• Place a marker 15 yards front and center of the goal.

• Each team has a supply of soccer balls placed nearby.

• A player from team 1 is positioned in goal as the goalkeeper.

PROCEDURE

1. The first player for team 2 sprints out from the goal post, around the marker placed 15 yards from goal.

2. As the first player nears the marker the second player in line for team 2 plays a rolling ball toward the penalty spot for his or her teammate to finish with a one-time shot.

3. After shooting at goal the player sprints to the goal line and positions themself as the goalkeeper while team 1 attempts to score in the same manner.

4. The first team to score 15 goals wins the contest.

COACHING TIPS

- Vary the type of service (e.g., rolling balls, bouncing balls, angled passes).

ONE-TOUCH FINISHING OF CROSSED BALLS

OBJECTIVES

- To finish balls served across the goal area

- To provide goalkeeper training

SETUP

- Play on one end of a field with a regulation goal.

- Position a goalkeeper in goal.

- Divide the team into two groups.

- One group (servers), each with a ball, are positioned on a sideline of the penalty area, about 5 yards from the end line of the field.

- The other group (shooters) is positioned front and center of the goal near to the penalty spot, 12 to 15 yards from goal.

PROCEDURE

1. The first player in the serving line plays a low, driven ball across the goalmouth, 6 to 8 yards out from the goal line.

2. The first player in the shooting line runs forward into the goalmouth to deflect/shoot the ball on goal.

3. All finishes must be one touch.

4. Goalkeeper attempts to save all shots.

5. After each shooter has taken six to ten shots the groups switch roles (i.e., servers become shooters and shooters become servers).

COACHING TIPS

- Emphasize the timing of the run into the goal area. The shooter should not arrive too early; rather he or she should be sprinting into the goalmouth just as the ball arrives.

SCORE FROM MULTIPLE SERVERS

sports-graphics.com

OBJECTIVES

- To shoot with power and accuracy using two touches to prepare and strike the ball

- To provide fitness training

- To provide goalkeeper training

SETUP

- Play within the penalty area with a full-sized goal on the end line.

- Place a marker at the center of the penalty arc, about 22 yards front and center of the goal.

- Station four servers, each with a supply of balls, around the perimeter of the penalty area.

- Number the servers 1, 2, 3, and 4.

- The shooter is positioned on the penalty arc next to the marker.

- The goalkeeper is stationed in the goal.

PROCEDURE

1. Server 1 passes a ball into the penalty area.

2. The shooter moves quickly to the ball, controls it toward goal with the first touch, and shoots to score with the second touch.

3. The shooter immediately returns to the marker, then sprints into the area to strike a ball played by server 2.

4. The goalkeeper attempts to save all shots.

5. The shooter continues through the four servers for two rounds of shots (eight consecutive shots).

6. The shooter then switches positions with one of the servers, and the round is repeated with a different shooter.

7. Continue until all players have taken two turns as the shooter.

COACHING TIPS

- As a variation, require first-time (one-touch) shooting.

1 VS 1 TO 2 VS 1 THROUGH THE CHANNEL

sports-graphics.com

OBJECTIVE

- To improve finishing skills

SETUP

- Play on one end of a field with full-sized goal on the end line.

- Place a marker on each side of the half arc at the top of the penalty area to form the channel.

- Designate three or four players as defenders, while the remaining players are attackers.

- One defender and one attacker (striker) position themselves within the penalty area.

- The remaining defenders are stationed behind the goal to await their turn.

- The remaining attackers, each with a ball, are positioned 25 yards front and center of goal.

PROCEDURE

1. The first attacker passes a ball through the channel to the striker positioned in the penalty area and follows the pass to join the striker to create a 2-vs-1 situation to goal.

2. Play continues until a shot on goal occurs or a defender wins the ball.

3. The original striker retrieves the ball and returns to the line of attackers.

4. The player who passed to the striker becomes the striker for the next round.

5. The defender plays for three consecutive rounds, then another defender takes his or her place.

COACHING TIPS

- Encourage the striker to use sudden changes of speed and direction to free him- or herself from the defender to receive the pass from the midfielder through the channel.

ATTACK TRANSITION TO DEFENSE

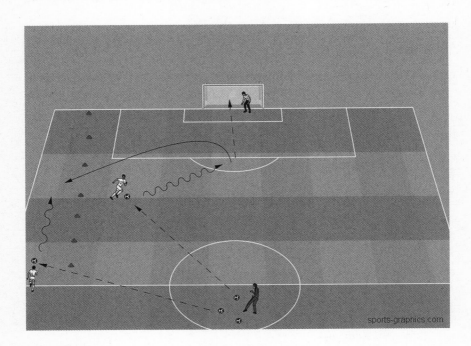

OBJECTIVES

- To sharpen shooting/finishing skills

- To practice immediate transition from attack to defense

SETUP

- Play on one end of a regulation field with a full-sized goal on the end line.

- Position a goalkeeper in goal.

- Position a server/passer 40 yards from goal with a supply of balls.

- Place markers to designate a 10-yard-wide channel the length of the touchline (sideline) nearest to the server.

- Position a player (dribbler) in the wide channel, 40 yards from goal.

- Position an attacker (shooter) about 25 yards from goal near to the wide channel.

PROCEDURE

1. The server initiates play by passing a ball to the attacker (shooter).

2. The attacker turns toward goal with the ball, dribbles 8 to 10 yards, and shoots to score.

3. As the attacker (shooter) releases the shot the server passes a ball to the player (dribbler) positioned in the wide channel.

4. The dribbler advances at speed toward the end line within the channel with the objective of reaching the end line before the shooter (now a defender) can prevent him or her from doing so.

5. The shooter, after releasing a shot at goal, makes an immediate transition to defense by sprinting into the wide channel to prevent the dribbler from advancing with the ball to the end line.

6. The round ends when the defender wins the ball or the dribbler advances over the end line with the ball.

7. The original shooter then rotates to the server/passer position, the original server moves to the channel as the dribbler, and the original dribbler becomes the shooter for the next round.

COACHING TIPS

- Reduce the distance from passer to shooter for younger players.

1 VS 1 TO GOAL

OBJECTIVES

- To compete 1 vs 1 within the penalty area

- To rehearse attacking and defending responsibilities in a 1-vs-1 situation

SETUP

- Place a marker about 25 yards front and center of the full-sized goal.

- Split the team into two groups (attackers and defenders).

- Position a goalkeeper in goal.

- Defending team players are positioned beside the goal with a supply of balls.

- Attacking team players are positioned at the marker 25 yards from goal.

PROCEDURE

1. The first defender passes a ball to the first attacker and moves out from the goal to defend.

2. The attacker attempts to beat the defender on the dribble before shooting at goal.

3. Award one point to the attacking team for each goal scored.

4. After each attempt the next defender immediately passes a ball to the next attacker and the play continues.

5. Each team attacks for five minutes and then defends for five minutes.

6. The team scoring the most points wins the competition.

COACHING TIPS

- This drill can be effectively used to practice both the offensive and defensive responsibilities in the 1-vs-1 situation.

- Encourage the attacker (dribbler) to use quick change of pace and direction to bypass the defending player to shoot at goal.

- The defending player should quickly close down the space to the dribbler and force the dribbler into a poor shooting angle.

2 VS 1 TO GOALS

OBJECTIVES

- To practice attacking in a numbers-up situation

- To use the give-and-go pass combination to bypass a single defender

- To practice defending in a numbers-down situation

SETUP

- Place markers to outline a 20-yard-wide by 30-yard-long field with a full-sized goal and goalkeeper on each end line.

- Divide the group into two teams who are stationed at opposite ends of the field.

- The coach (server) is positioned on the sideline with a supply of balls.

PROCEDURE

1. The coach passes a ball to either team to initiate play.

2. Two players from that team immediately move forward to attack the opponents' goal.

3. One player on the opposing team immediately steps out to defend, creating a 2-vs-1 situation to goal.

4. Play continues until a goal is scored, the defender wins the ball, or the ball travels out of the field area. Players then return to their respective end lines.

5. The coach immediately serves another ball to initiate the next 2-vs-1 competition.

COACHING TIPS

- Encourage the first attacker (player with ball) to dribble at and commit the defender before passing the ball to his or her partner (second attacker).

1 VS 2 TO GOAL

OBJECTIVE

- To create and finish scoring opportunities in a numbers-down (1-vs-2) situation

SETUP

- Play within the penalty area with a regulation goal positioned on the endline.

- Station a neutral goalkeeper in goal who attempts to save all shots.

- Form teams of two players each.

PROCEDURE

1. One team of two players is stationed within the penalty area.

2. One player from the opposing team is also positioned within the area, to assume the role of a single attacker.

3. The attacker's partner (server) stations outside the penalty area with a supply of six balls.

4. The neutral goalkeeper is stationed in goal and attempts to save all shots.

5. Play begins with the server kicking a ball to his or her teammate stationed within the penalty area.

6. The player receiving the ball attempts to score by evading the two opponents (defenders) and shooting the ball past the goalkeeper.

7. Immediately after a score, or a save by the goalkeeper, or the ball going out of play, the server plays another ball into the area and play continues.

8. Play for 90 seconds, after which the server switches places with his or her teammate and repeats the round.

9. Play a series of 90-second rounds, with teams switching roles (attack and defense) every two rounds.

10. Award one point for a shot on goal saved by the goalkeeper, and two points for a goal scored. Teammates total their points scored to get the team score. The team scoring the most points wins the game.

COACHING TIPS

*   Adjust the size of the playing area to accommodate the age and ability of players.

2 VS 2 IN THE PENALTY AREA

OBJECTIVE

- To combine with a teammate to create and finish scoring opportunities

SETUP

- Form teams of two players each.

- Position a goalkeeper in goal.

- Coach (server) stands at the top of the penalty area with a supply of balls.

- Two teams enter the penalty area for the first round of play.

PROCEDURE

1. The coach kicks a ball into the penalty area.

2. Both teams compete for possession.

3. The team that gains possession of the ball attacks the goal and attempts to score; the opponents defend.

4. Roles immediately reverse upon change of possession.

5. After a shot on goal or ball out of bounds the coach immediately plays another ball into the area and play continues.

6. Play each round for 60 seconds at maximum effort, then two different teams enter the area and repeat.

COACHING TIPS

*   Players should combine with their teammate to create a scoring opportunity.

*   Defensive players should force opponents into poor shooting positions.

TRANSITION 3 VS 2 TO 2 VS 1

sports-graphics.com

OBJECTIVES

- To practice attacking in numbers-up situations

- To practice defending when outnumbered

SETUP

- Play on a 30-yard-long by 20-yard-wide field with a full-sized goal centered on each end line.

- A goalkeeper is stationed in each goal.

- Organize two teams (1 and 2) of five to seven players each.

- Use colored vests to differentiate teams.

- Teams are positioned on the same end of the field, with one team on each side of the goal.

- Position two players from team 2 to defend goal B.

- Place a supply of balls inside each goal.

- Team 1 has the ball to begin.

PROCEDURE

1. Three players from team 1 advance off their end line to attack goal B which is defended by two players from team 2 and a goalkeeper.

2. After a shot on goal, or a shot traveling over the end line, or a ball stolen by a defender, the goalkeeper in goal B immediately distributes a ball to the original two defenders (team 2), who then attack goal A.

3. One of the three original attackers from team 1 remains on the field to defend goal A to create a 2-vs-1 player advantage for team 2 as they counterattack goal A.

4. The other 2 players from team 1 remain near the end line (of goal B) to defend goal B in the next round.

5. Immediately after an attempt on goal A, three players from team 2 advance off the line to attack goal B, which is now defended by two players from team 1.

6. The drill continues as teams attack goal B in a 3-vs-2 situation and counterattack goal A in a 2-vs-1 situation.

COACHING TIPS

- Emphasize immediate transition from attack to defense and vice versa.

NATIONS CUP TOURNAMENT

sports-graphics.com

OBJECTIVE

- To develop shooting skills under pressure of limited time, restricted space, and challenging opponents

SETUP

- Each player pairs up with a teammate.

- Play within the penalty area of a regulation field with the goal centered on the end line.

- Place a supply of balls inside the goal.

- Organize three teams of two players each.

- Each team chooses a country to represent (e.g., USA, England, Germany).

- All teams are positioned within the penalty area.

- The goalkeeper is positioned in the goal.

PROCEDURE

1. The drill begins as the goalkeeper tosses two balls toward the outer edge of the penalty area.

2. All teams vie for possession.

3. The teams gaining possession of a ball attempt to score; the other team defends.

4. After each save or score the goalkeeper immediately returns a ball into play by tossing it toward the edge of the penalty area.

5. When a team scores a goal the two teammates shout out their country name or the score does not count.

6. Play a series of three-minute rounds.

7. The team that scores the most goals through all rounds is the champion.

COACHING TIPS

- Encourage players to combine with teammates to create scoring opportunities.

- Prohibit slide tackles.

3 VS 2 TO FULL GOALS

sports-graphics.com

OBJECTIVE

*   To practice attacking in a numbers-up situation and defending in a numbers-down situation

SETUP

*   Divide the group into two teams.

*   Play on a 30-yard-long by 20-yard-wide field, with a full-sized goal (and goalkeeper) on each end line.

*   Teams are positioned on opposite ends of the field;

*   The coach acts as the server and is stationed with a supply of balls near to the midline.

PROCEDURE

1. Coach serves a ball to one of the teams.

2. Three players from that team immediately advance off their end line to attack the opponent's goal.

3. Two players from the opposing team immediately advance off of their end line to defend, creating a 3-vs-2 situation.

4. Play continues until a shot at goal, a goal scored, or the ball out of play.

5. The coach then serves a ball for the next 3-vs-2 competition.

6. Teams alternate playing on attack and defense.

COACHING TIPS

- The attacking team should use their player advantage to create scoring opportunities.

- The defending team must protect the most dangerous space and try to limit attacking options.

TRANSITION 4 VS 2 TO 2 VS 4

OBJECTIVE

- To create and finish scoring opportunities through combination play

SETUP

- Use markers to outline a field area of 50 yards long by 30 yards wide bisected by a midline.

- Designate two teams of six field players and one goalkeeper.

- Position a regulation goal on opposite end lines.

- Designate four attackers and two defenders for each team.

- The four attackers are positioned in the opponent's half of the field; the two defenders are stationed in their own half (i.e., nearest to the goal they are defending), creating a 4-vs-2 situation in each half.

- Station a goalkeeper in each goal; use colored vests to differentiate teams.
- Award one goalkeeper possession of the ball to begin.

PROCEDURE

1. The goalkeeper initiates play by distributing the ball to a teammate (attacker) in the opposite half of the field.

2. Each team defends a goal and can score on the opponent's goal.

3. Attackers and defenders are restricted to movement within their designated half of the field.

4. A defender who wins the ball initiates a counterattack by passing to a teammate (attacker) in the opposite half of the field.

5. After making a save the goalkeeper distributes the ball to a teammate (either a defender or an attacker in the opposite half) and play continues.

6. Play for 15 to 20 minutes.

7. The team scoring the most goals wins the game.

COACHING TIPS

- As a variation, impose restrictions on players; for example, limit touches allowed to receive and pass the ball, or require that all goals must be scored on first-time (one-touch) shots.

FINISHING CROSSES

OBJECTIVES

- To practice serving balls into the penalty area from wide areas

- To finish crosses served from wide areas

SETUP

- Play on one end of a regulation field with a full-sized goal on the end line.

- Place a marker on each touchline about 40 yards from the goal line.

- Position three players, each with a ball, at the markers 40 yards from goal.

- Position an additional marker on each side of the half arc at the top of the penalty area.

- Position two strikers at the markers on each side of the half arc.

- Position a goalkeeper in goal who attempts to save all shots.

PROCEDURE

1. To initiate play, one of the flank players dribbles at speed toward the end line and serves a ball into the penalty area.

2. At the same time the first two strikers make penetrating runs toward the goal and attempt to finish the crossed ball.

3. After each attempt at goal the next pair of strikers and opposite flank player do likewise.

4. Players return to their original positions after each attempt at goal.

5. Alternate serves from the right and left flanks.

COACHING TIPS

- Emphasize proper timing of the striker runs into the penalty area.

GAME WITH NEUTRAL WINGERS

OBJECTIVES

• To develop effective flank play

• To improve player ability to finish (score) balls crossed into the penalty area from wide areas

SETUP

• Form two teams of four players and one goalkeeper.

• Play on a 50-yard-wide by 60-yard-long field area, with a full-sized goal centered on each end line.

• Place markers to designate a channel 5 yards wide on each flank, extending the length of the field.

- Designate two additional players as neutral wingers, one positioned in each flank channel, who join with the team in possession of the ball.

- Station a goalkeeper in each goal,

- One ball is required per game. An extra supply of balls should be placed behind each goal.

PROCEDURE

1. Begin with a kickoff from the center of the field. Teams play 4 vs 4 in the 40-yard-wide middle channel.

2. Each team defends a goal and can score in the opponents' goal.

3. The neutral wingers positioned in the flank channel always join the team with possession to create a 6-vs-4 player advantage for the attacking team; the neutral wingers do not defend.

4. Goals can be scored directly from shots originating in the middle channel, or from balls crossed into the goal area by the neutral wingers.

5. Neutral wingers are restricted to movement within their flank channel; they are not permitted to enter the central channel.

6. When a neutral winger receives a ball passed from a central player or the goalkeeper, he or she is required to immediately dribble at top speed within the flank channel toward the opponents' end line and cross the ball into the goal area. Otherwise, regular soccer rules apply.

7. Award one point for each goal scored from a shot originating within the central channel, and two points for a goal scored directly off a crossed ball.

8. Play for 20 minutes. The team scoring the most points wins the match.

COACHING TIPS

- This drill reinforces the use of flank play to attack an opponent's defense. It also provides training for the goalkeeper in handling lofted balls served into the goal area.

TEAM THAT SCORES STAYS

OBJECTIVES

- To create and finish scoring opportunities
- To improve fitness

SETUP

- Play on one end of a regulation field with a full-sized goal on the end line.
- Place markers to double the depth of the penalty area, creating a field area 36 yards deep and 44 yards wide.
- Organize three teams of four players each.
- Use colored vests to differentiate teams.
- Station one team within the field area; this team will start as the defending team and positions to defend the goal.

- Station one team on the opposite end line facing the goal, with possession of the ball. This team will begin as the attacking team.

- Players from the third team spread themselves around the perimeter of the field to serve as passing outlets for the team with the ball, thus creating an 8-vs-4 player advantage for the team with possession.

- The goalkeeper is neutral and attempts to save all shots.

PROCEDURE

1. The team with the ball enters the field to attack the opponent's goal; the opponents defend.

2. Players from the third team who are positioned around the perimeter of the field (neutrals) are allowed to move laterally along the perimeter lines to receive passes but cannot enter the field area.

3. The team with possession can pass to the neutral players who must use three or fewer touches to return the ball to a central player.

4. Change of possession occurs when the ball leaves the field area, after a goal is scored, or when a defender wins the ball.

5. If the goalkeeper saves a shot on goal, he or she tosses the ball toward the far corner of the field and teams compete for possession.

6. Play is continuous with the two competing teams alternating from attack to defense with each change of possession.

7. After a goal scored the team conceding the goal leaves the field and its players assume the role of neutral player positioned on the perimeter.

8. The team that scored stays on the field to play another round.

9. The team whose players were originally serving as neutrals enter the field to compete against the team that won the previous game.

COACHING TIPS

- Emphasize the attacking concepts of width, depth, and penetration.

- Emphasize the defensive principles of pressure (first defender), cover (second defender), and balance (third defender).

1 VS 1 THROUGH 3 VS 3 FINISHING

OBJECTIVES

- To create and finish scoring opportunities

- To defend on an individual and group basis

SETUP

- Play on a 30-yard-by-25-yard field area with a full-sized goal centered on each end line.

- Designate two teams of three players each.

- Teams (players) station themselves on their respective end lines, each with a ball.

- Position a goalkeeper in each goal.

- The coach positions near the midline of the field with a supply of balls.

PROCEDURE

1. One player from each of the teams, without a ball, moves within the field area.

2. The coach initiates play by passing a ball to one of those players.

3. Those two players compete 1 vs 1 until a shot on goal or the ball leaves the field area.

4. At that moment one player from the team that was defending last enters the field with a ball to join his or her teammate to attack the opponent's goal 2 vs 1.

5. After a shot on goal or ball out of bounds a teammate of the player who was defending numbers down (1-vs-2) passes a ball to him/her and enters the field to create a 2-vs-2 situation toward the opposite goal.

6. Continue adding a player to the drill with each shot on goal or ball out of bounds to progress through 3-vs-2 and 3-vs-3 competition.

7. The team that scores the most goals at the end of the 3-vs-3 competition wins the round.

8. Repeat several rounds of 1-vs-1 through 3-vs-3 competition.

COACHING TIPS

- Emphasize key points when attacking and defending in an outnumbered situation.

ATTACKER VS DEFENDER

sports-graphics.com

OBJECTIVE

* To practice shooting off the dribble while being challenged by an opponent

SETUP

* Play on one end of a regulation field with a full-sized goal on the end line.

* Position a goalkeeper in goal.

* Place markers 25 yards and 30 yards front and center of the goal.

* One player (shooter) is positioned at the marker 25 yards from goal with their back to goal.

* All other players (servers). each with a ball, are positioned in a single-file line facing the goal at the marker 30 yards from goal.

PROCEDURE

1. The first player in the server line passes a ball toward goal, a few feet past the shooter.

2. The shooter immediately turns, collects the ball, dribbles at speed toward goal, and releases a shot from 12 to 15 yards of distance.

3. The player who passed the ball immediately assumes the role of defender and chases the dribbler to prevent a shot on goal.

4. After the attempt on goal the shooter returns to the server line and the chasing defender becomes the next shooter.

COACHING TIPS

*   Encourage the attacker to turn quickly, dribble at speed, and release the shot.

FAST AND FURIOUS

OBJECTIVES

- To finish (score) balls crossed into the goal mouth from wide areas

- To provide goalkeeper training for defending crossed balls

SETUP

- Play on one end of a regulation field with a goal.

- Position a goalkeeper in goal.

- Position two markers at the top edge of the penalty area, one on each side of the half arc.

- Position two forwards (strikers) at each marker.

- Position two flank players, each with a supply of balls, on opposite touchlines, about 25 yards from the end line.

PROCEDURE

1. The first player on one flank dribbles at speed toward the end line and crosses a ball into the goal mouth.

2. Two strikers time their runs into the box and attempt to score the crossed ball.

3. Goalkeeper tries to save all shots.

4. Immediately after each attempt on goal a flank player on the opposite sideline repeats the drill.

5. Alternate crosses from one flank and the other.

6. Continue at a fast pace until each pair of strikers have attempted to finish ten or more balls crossed into the goal area.

COACHING TIPS

- Encourage strikers to time their runs into the goalmouth so as not to arrive too early.

SECTION 5
HEADING

Soccer is the only sport in which players literally use their heads to propel the ball. Heading skills are used for offensive as well as defending purposes, so mastery of the aerial game is essential for all field players. Three basic heading techniques—jump header, dive header, and flick header—are commonly observed in game competition. Each is used for slightly different situations.

The jump header is most often used when competing with an opponent who is also trying to head the ball. To perform the technique, use a two-footed takeoff to jump upward, arch the upper body back from the vertical, and then snap forward at the waist to contact the ball on the flat surface of the forehead. Opportunities to score goals that require proper execution of the jump header can arise from corner kicks, free kicks, and even long throw-ins. When heading to score the ball should be directed downward toward the goal line as that is the most difficult save for the goalkeeper to make. The jump header can also be used for defensive purposes such as clearing a ball flighted into the defending team's goal area. In that situation the clearance should be directed high, far, and toward the flank area of the field, away from the most dangerous scoring zone front and center of the goal.

The dive header is an acrobatic skill that is sometimes used to score spectacular goals from low balls traveling across the goal mouth. The dive header can also be used by defending players to re-direct a driven ball out and away from the goal area. To perform the dive header a player should vault forward parallel to the ground with head tilted back and neck firm. The ball is contacted on the flat surface of the forehead, with arms and hands extended forward and downward to break the fall to the ground.

The flick header is a third possible heading option, designed primarily to alter the flight path of the ball while allowing it to continue in the same general direction. To perform the flick header the player moves to a position to intercept the flight path of the ball, then allows the ball to glance off the top of the forehead. This action creates a slight and sudden change in the flight trajectory, which can unbalance and pose problems for defending players.

IMPORTANT NOTE ON HEADING

In recent years there has been much discussion and some concern over the issue that repetitive heading of a soccer ball, particularly at the youth level, may potentially result in long-term harmful effects on brain structure and function. While there has been no concrete evidence presented to confirm that this is definitely the case, major soccer organizations worldwide recognize this concern and have responded by instituting general heading guidelines for youth players. For example, U.S. Soccer has issued a mandate on heading the ball in training and competitions for several age groups. The mandate applies to players 12 years and younger and became effective January 1, 2016. According to the mandate, players 10 years old or younger cannot be taught the skill of heading and cannot intentionally head the ball in a competitive game. Players who are 11 and 12 years old can receive heading instruction in training, but instruction is limited to 30 minutes per week. However, 11 and 12 year olds are allowed to head the ball in game competition. In the event a U10 or younger player deliberately heads the ball on the field, the opposing team will be awarded an indirect free kick at the spot of the foul. If the header occurs in the goal box area, the ball will be placed outside the box.

The Union of European Football Associations (UEFA) has proposed similar guidelines on how to manage heading during practices and matches. Because opinions on this matter may vary somewhat from one country to another, UEFA encourages National Associations to institute these guidelines as a minimum as it is acknowledged that scientific evidence at this moment does not allow for more detailed guidelines. The overall aim of UEFA's Heading Guidelines is to limit heading in youth soccer (football) to what is deemed necessary for the promotion of the game.

The FA (Football Association), English football's governing body, has also instituted heading guidelines for youth participating in English football. For more detailed information on the UEFA and FA guidelines, visit the following websites:

FA Guidelines

UEFA Guidelines

Note: The QR code web addresses were current as of June 2024.

FUNDAMENTAL HEADING

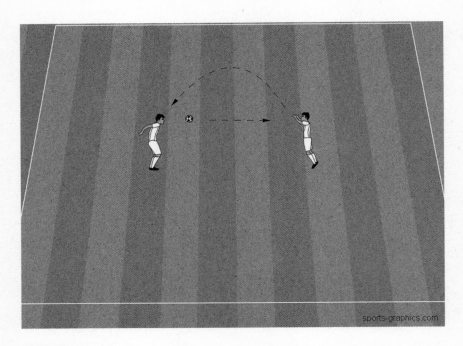

OBJECTIVE

- To rehearse the fundamental heading technique

SETUP

- Players pair up with a partner.

- Partners face one another, 3 yards apart.

- One player (server) has a ball.

PROCEDURE

1. The server tosses the ball toward the partner at head height.

2. The partner arches back from the waist, then snaps the upper body forward, and contacts the ball on the flat surface of the forehead.

3. The server catches the headed ball and repeats the action.

4. Continue until the player has headed 15 to 20 tosses back to the server.

COACHING TIPS

• Emphasize the importance of arching backward from the waist, then snapping forward with head and neck held firm as the ball contacts the forehead.

PARTNER HEAD JUGGLE

OBJECTIVE

- To develop confidence in contacting the ball on the flat surface of the forehead

SETUP

- Players pair up with a partner.

- Partners face one another, 2–3 yards apart.

- One partner has the ball.

PROCEDURE

1. The player with the ball initiates the drill by tossing it upward toward the partner.

2. Partners attempt to head the ball back and forth for as many touches as possible without letting the ball drop to the ground.

3. Keep count of number of consecutive headers.

4. Players may only use their head to keep the ball airborne—no feet allowed!

5. If the ball drops to the ground the players must restart their count at zero.

6. The pair who keep the ball airborne for the most consecutive headers wins the competition.

COACHING TIPS

*   Encourage players to contact the ball on the flat surface of the forehead, directing it toward the partner.

*   Players should bend slightly at the knees with eyes open and mouth closed, as the ball contacts their forehead.

TOSS, JUMP, HEAD, SCORE

sports-graphics.com

OBJECTIVE

- To improve the jump header technique

SETUP

- Form groups of three players each.

- Place markers to outline an area 10 by 12 yards for each group.

- Position a small goal (3 to 4 yards wide) at one end of the area.

- One player stands in the goal as the goalkeeper.

- One player takes a position beside the goal as the server.

- The third player, who will be heading the ball, is positioned 10 yards front and center of the goal.

- One ball is required; place a supply of balls near the server.

PROCEDURE

1. The server initiates play by tossing a ball upward so that it drops near the center of the area.

2. The player heading the ball moves forward and attempts to score by jumping upward and heading it past the goalkeeper.

3. Players rotate positions after each header and repeat the drill. The original server assumes the role of goalkeeper, the goalkeeper rotates to the header position, and the original header becomes the server for the next round.

4. Play until each player has attempted 15 to 20 headers on goal.

5. Award two points for a goal scored and one point for a header on goal saved by the keeper.

6. The player who scores the most points wins the heading competition.

COACHING TIPS

- Encourage players to jump early and head the ball downward toward a corner of the goal.

- Emphasize proper heading technique (upper body arched back from the vertical, chin tucked, neck firm, ball contacted on forehead).

- Allow younger players to head the ball with both feet on the ground (i.e., without jumping upward).

JUMP, HEAD, DO IT AGAIN

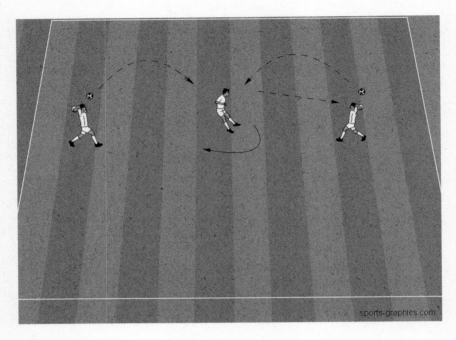

OBJECTIVES

- To improve jump header technique
- To improve fitness

SETUP

- Organize groups of three players each.
- Two players in the group (servers) face one another, 10 yards apart, each with a ball.
- The third player stands midway between the two servers.

PROCEDURE

1. Server 1 tosses a ball slightly above head height toward the central player who jumps upward and heads the ball directly back to the server.

2. The player immediately turns 180 degrees to jump and head a ball tossed by server 2.

3. Continue for 30 consecutive headers, alternating from one server to the other, after which the central player exchanges places with one of the servers and the drill is repeated.

4. Continue until each player has taken a minimum of two turns heading the ball.

COACHING TIPS

- Encourage players to jump vertically upward (not forward), arch their upper trunk back prior to the ball's arrival, and snap forward to contact the ball with their forehead.

- Players should keep their head steady, eyes open, and mouth closed upon contact with the ball.

TEAM HEADING RACE

OBJECTIVE

• To improve heading technique in a competitive, fun-filled exercise

SETUP

• Form teams of four to six players each.

• Teams are positioned side-by-side in single file line with 3 yards of distance between the lines.

• Players in each line maintain at least 2 feet distance from their teammates.

• One player for each team is designated as the server who is positioned 2 yards in front of the team, facing the first player in line.

• Each server has a ball.

PROCEDURE

1. On the command "Begin the race," each server tosses a ball at head height to the first player in their team's line.

2. The player heads the ball back to the server and immediately assumes a kneeling position.

3. The server then tosses the ball to the second player in line who heads to the server and kneels.

4. Servers continue through the line of teammates until all players have headed to the server and are kneeling.

5. The team whose players are all kneeling first wins the race.

6. Players then stand and rotate positions in preparation for the next round.

7. The original server moves to the back of the line, the first player in the line becomes the server, and everyone else moves one spot forward.

8. The first team to win three races wins the competition.

COACHING TIPS

*   Remind players that while they should complete the heading race as quickly as possible, they should not sacrifice proper heading technique for speed.

CLEAR IT AWAY

OBJECTIVE

- To improve the technique used for defensive heading (clearing a ball high and far)

SETUP

- Play on one end of a field with a full-sized goal on the end line.

- Divide the group into two teams.

- Position one team (headers) next to one of the goal posts (without soccer balls).

- Position the other group (servers), each with a ball, within the penalty arc at the top of the penalty area.

- No goalkeeper is necessary in this drill.

PROCEDURE

1. The first server tosses a high ball toward the penalty spot.

2. The first player in the heading group moves forward from the goal post and attempts to head the ball high and far so that it drops to the ground outside of the penalty area.

3. Award the player one point for a headed clearance that lands outside of the penalty area.

4. Continue until each player has taken five attempts at heading a flighted ball out of the penalty area.

5. Teams then switch roles and repeat.

6. The team that totals the most points wins the heading competition.

COACHING TIPS

*   Encourage players to jump early, arch back at the waist, and snap forward as the ball arrives.

HEAD IT HOME

sports-graphics.com

OBJECTIVE

- To score from headers

SETUP

- Play on one end of the field with a regulation goal.

- Station a goalkeeper in goal.

- Position a server at each goal post.

- Each server has four soccer balls nearby.

- Players pair up with a partner for heading competition.

- The first pair positions themselves 15 yards front and center of the goal.

PROCEDURE

1. On command the first player runs toward goal.

2. One of the servers tosses a ball just above head height toward the center of the 6-yard box.

3. The advancing player jumps upward, arches back at the waist, and attempts to head the ball past the goalkeeper.

4. The player immediately returns to the penalty spot and his partner repeats the drill with the opposite server.

5. Partners continue heading to score, alternating from one server to the other, until the supply of balls is exhausted.

6. The player scoring the most goals wins the scoring contest.

COACHING TIPS

- Encourage players to jump early, then snap forward from the waist, and contact the ball on the flat surface of the forehead.

- Keep neck and head firmly positioned at the moment of contact.

HEADERS ONLY

sports-graphics.com

OBJECTIVE

- To score from headers in a small-sided situation

SETUP

- Play within an area 40 yards wide by 50 yards long.

- Position a full-sized goal at the center of each end line.

- Organize two teams of five to seven players each.

- Designate three additional neutral players, who always join the team in possession of the ball.

- Use colored vests to differentiate teams and the neutral players.

- Award one team possession of the ball to begin.

- No goalkeepers are required.

PROCEDURE

1. Each team defends a goal and scores in the opponent's goal.

2. Passing among teammates is accomplished by throwing and catching the ball with the hands rather than using foot skills.

3. Players may take up to five steps with the ball before passing it to a teammate.

4. Violation of the five-step rule results in loss of possession to the opposing team.

5. Neutral players joining with the team in possession create a three-player advantage for the attacking team.

6. Although there are no designated goalkeepers all players are permitted to use their hands to intercept passes or block shots at their goal.

7. Goals are scored only by heading a ball tossed by a teammate through the opponent's goal.

8. Defending players gain possession of the ball by intercepting an opponent's pass, when an opponent drops the ball to the ground, when an opponent takes more than five steps with the ball, or when the ball is played out of bounds by an opponent.

9. Play for 15 to 20 minutes.

10. The team scoring the most header goals wins the contest.

COACHING TIPS

- Player movement, both offensively and defensively, should simulate the patterns and positioning used in an actual match.

- Encourage team members to attack and defend as a group.

- Emphasize that the ball should be headed on a downward plane toward the goal line when attempting to score from a header.

SCORING FROM DIVE HEADERS

sports-graphics.com

OBJECTIVE

*   To improve the dive header technique

SETUP

*   Play on one end of a regulation field with a full-sized goal.

*   Divide the group into teams of equal numbers.

*   Teams position side by side in single file, about 15 yards from the goal.

*   Station a server 6 yards to each side of the goal, about 6 yards out from the end line.

*   Each server has a supply of balls.

*   The neutral goalkeeper positions in goal.

PROCEDURE

1. Servers alternate tossing a ball parallel to the ground at a height of 3 to 4 feet into the area front and center of the goal.

2. Teams (players) alternate attempting to score a diving header by running forward and launching themselves through the air parallel to the ground to meet the ball.

3. The goalkeeper attempts to save all shots.

4. Continue until each player has attempted at least five dive headers.

5. Award two points for a goal scored and one point for a ball on goal saved by the goalkeeper.

COACHING TIPS

- Proper dive heading technique is essential to prevent injury. Encourage players to dive forward parallel to the ground with head tilted back and neck firm.

- The ball is contacted on the flat surface of the forehead, with eyes open and mouth closed.

- Arms are extended forward and downward to cushion the impact with the ground.

- This drill is **not recommended** for younger players (10 years and under) who lack adequate strength and coordination.

SECTION 6
INDIVIDUAL AND GROUP
TACTICS

Mastery of the various passing, dribbling, shooting, and heading skills provide a foundation for improved soccer performance. That said, skill proficiency is not the only requirement necessary to compete at higher levels of competition. Players must also develop an understanding of when, where, and how to use those skills to best advantage, and that is where tactics come into play. Individual as well as team performance is largely dependent on the decisions players make in response to the ever-changing situations confronted during the match. Poor decisions often lead to individual mistakes and may ultimately result in goals scored against the team.

The drills described in section 6 require players to execute soccer-specific skills while making split-second decisions with respect to the best course of action (e.g., when and where to move, pass, dribble, shoot) for a given situation. Players will discover by trial and error as well as from feedback from the coach what works best and what doesn't in a specific situation.

1 VS 1 ATTACK AND DEFEND

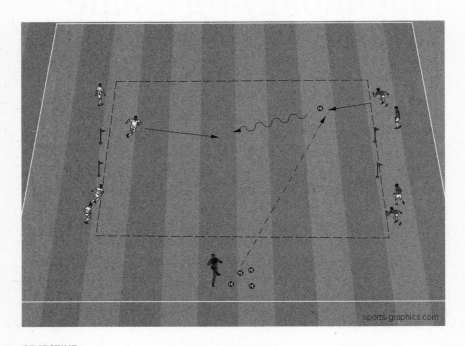

sports-graphics.com

OBJECTIVE

- To practice individual attacking and defending tactics

SETUP

- Divide the group into two teams of four to six players each.

- Label players on each team with a number, beginning with 1 and progressing through the number of players on the team.

- Position markers to outline a 20-yard-long by 15-yard-wide field.

- Place markers to represent a 3-yard-wide goal at each end of the field.

- The coach is positioned at the midline of the field with a supply of balls.

- Teams position themselves on opposite ends of the field.

- Each team defends the goal on its end line and can score by passing the ball into the opponents' goal.

- Do not use goalkeepers.

PROCEDURE

1. The coach calls out a number, for example 3.

2. That player for each team sprints on to the field.

3. The coach passes a ball to the first player to enter the field.

4. Those two players compete 1 vs 1 until a score or the ball goes out of the field area.

5. The coach then calls out another number, and the process is repeated with those two players.

6. Repeat until each player has played several 1-vs-1 matchups.

7. The team scoring the most goals wins.

COACHING POINTS

- Encourage players to make the immediate transition from attack to defense and vice versa upon change of possession.

2 VS 1 + 1

OBJECTIVES

- To attack and defend in a 2-vs-1 situation

- To practice the wall pass combination with a teammate to bypass a single defender

- To practice immediate transition from attack to defense and vice versa upon change of possession

SETUP

- Organize teams of two players each.

- Use markers to create a 15-yard-wide by 20-yard-long field for each game.

- Position flags or similar markers to represent a 4-yard-wide goal at the center of each end line.

PROCEDURE

1. Award one team possession of the ball to begin.

2. Each team defends the goal on its end line.

3. The team with possession attacks the opponent's goal with two players; the defending team drops one player back as the goalkeeper and the other becomes a single defender to create a 2 vs 1 plus goalkeeper situation.

4. Change of possession occurs when the defender wins the ball, the goalkeeper makes a save, the ball goes out of the field area last touched by an attacker, or after a goal is scored.

5. If the defending player gains possession of the ball then he or she must first pass it back to their goalkeeper before the team can counterattack with both players.

6. After receiving the ball, either from a teammate's pass back or when making a save, the goalkeeper moves forward to join his or her teammate to create a 2-vs-1 attack on the opponent's goal.

7. One player on the team that lost possession of the ball immediately drops back to play as goalkeeper while his or her teammate plays as the single defender.

8. Teammates alternate turns playing as the goalkeeper with each change of possession.

9. Play for 10 to 15 minutes and keep a tally of goals scored.

10. The team scoring the most points wins the game.

COACHING TIPS

- Place an emphasis on immediate transition from attack to defense and vice versa upon each change of possession.

- Encourage attackers to dribble at the single defender and execute the wall (give-and-go) pass with their teammate to penetrate past the defender.

2 VS 2 + 4 POSSESSION

OBJECTIVE

- To use dribbling and passing skills to keep possession of the ball from outnumbered opponents

SETUP

- Form teams of two players each.

- Position markers to outline a 25-yard square playing area.

- Four teams (total of eight players) are involved in the drill.

- Two teams (four players) station themselves within the playing area.

- Award one team possession of the ball.

- Players from the other two teams position themselves as support players, one on each sideline.

PROCEDURE

1. Teams compete 2 vs 2 within the area with the objective of keeping possession of the ball from opponents.

2. Support players positioned on the sidelines join the team with possession to create a 6-vs-2 player advantage for that team.

3. Support players are permitted to move laterally along their sideline but are not allowed to move inward into the field area.

4. Support players are limited to three or fewer touches to receive and pass the ball.

5. Support players may receive the ball from, and pass it to, the central players only; support players may not pass among themselves.

6. Loss of possession occurs when a defending player steals the ball or when the ball goes out of play.

7. Play for five minutes after which the four central players switch roles with the four support players.

8. Play a total of four rounds with each team playing two rounds as support players and two rounds as central players.

9. Award one point for six or more passes without possession loss.

10. The team scoring the most points in a five-minute round wins the round.

COACHING TIPS

- To make the game more challenging for advanced players the coach can impose restrictions. For example, limit the support players to one-touch passes to return the ball to the team that passed it to them.

- Reduce the area size for young players.

2 VS 1 TO TARGET

OBJECTIVE

• To attack and defend in a 2-vs-1 situation

SETUP

• Form two teams of two players each.

• Use markers to outline a 10-yard-wide by 20-yard-long field area for each game.

• Teams position themselves on opposite ends of the field.

• Award one team possession of the ball.

PROCEDURE

1. Team with the ball initiates play by passing to their opponents positioned at the opposite end line of the field.

2. One player from the team that had the ball moves forward off the end line as a defender.

3. His or her teammate remains at the end line as a target.

4. The two opponents receive the ball and advance to take on (dribble at) the defender in a 2-vs-1 situation.

5. The attackers attempt to bypass the defender, either via the dribble or by executing a give-and-go pass, and then complete a pass to the target player positioned on the endline

6. Attackers score one point by completing a pass to their opponent's target player.

7. Attacking players must stay within the 10-yard-wide channel when attempting to advance with the ball past the defender.

8. The round ends when the defender steals the ball or when the attackers complete a pass to target, whichever occurs first.

9. The defending player scores one point for dispossessing an attacker or for forcing the attackers to play the ball out of the area.

10. After a point scored players return to their original positions on the end lines and repeat the round.

11. Play to ten points, after which teams switch roles (defend or attack) and repeat.

COACHING TIPS

*   Encourage attackers to dribble at (commit) the defender and then combine with teammate to execute a give-and-go pass to beat the defender.

3 VS 2 + ROTATING GOALKEEPER

sports-graphics.com

OBJECTIVE

- To practice group attack and defense in a numbers-up and numbers-down situation

SETUP

- Form two teams of three players each.

- Place markers to form a 15-yard-wide by 20-yard-long field with a 4-yard-wide goal centered on each end line.

- Award one team possession of the ball.

PROCEDURE

1. The team in possession of the ball attacks with three players; their opponents defend with two field players and a goalkeeper.

2. A team scores one point by passing the ball directly to the opposing goalkeeper.

3. The two defending players attempt to win the ball and/or deny penetrating passes to their goalkeeper.

4. If a defending player wins the ball he or she must first pass it back to their goalkeeper before the team can attack the opponent's goal.

5. Once the goalkeeper has possession of the ball she or he becomes a field player and moves forward to join his or her teammates in a three-player attack.

6. One player from the team that lost possession (defending team) immediately retreats into their goal to play as the goalkeeper.

7. Change of possession occurs when a defending player wins the ball, after a point is scored, or when the ball leaves the playing field.

8. Teammates alternate playing as goalkeeper with each change of possession.

COACHING TIPS

- Encourage immediate transition from attack to defense and vice versa upon change of possession.

3-VS-1 TRANSITION TO 1 VS 3

sports-graphics.com

OBJECTIVE

- To practice immediate transition from attack to defense and vice versa upon change of possession

SETUP

- Organize teams of three players each.

- Two teams play within a 30-yard-long by 15-yard-wide field area divided by a midline.

- Differentiate teams by colored vests.

- The coach is stationed near the midline of the field with a supply of balls.

- Teams position themselves in opposite halves of the field.

PROCEDURE

1. The coach passes a ball to one of the teams to initiate play.

2. The opposing team sends one player into that half of the field to win the ball.

3. The team with possession attempts to keep the ball from the opponent (defender) through the use of dribbling and passing skills.

4. If the defender wins possession, then he or she immediately passes the ball to a teammate in the opposite half of the field and sprints across the midline to joins his or her teammates.

5. One player from the team that lost possession sprints into the opponent's half of the field to regain possession, creating a 3-vs-1 situation in that half of the field.

6. If the ball is kicked out of the field area the coach immediately enters another ball.

7. Play is continuous with the ball switching location from one half of the field to the other with each change of possession.

COACHING TIPS

*   Emphasize the importance of quick transition from attack to defense and vice versa.

5-VS-3 TRANSITION TO 3 VS 5

sports-graphics.com

OBJECTIVE

- To maintain possession of the ball from outnumbered opponents in a restricted area

SETUP

- Position markers to outline a 30-by-20-yard area divided by a midline.

- Form two teams of five players each.

- Teams position themselves in opposite halves of the field.

- Coach is positioned beside the field with a supply of balls.

PROCEDURE

1. The coach passes a ball to a player on one of the teams.

2. The opposing team sends three players (defenders) into that half of the field to win the ball from the five opponents who attempt to keep possession.

3. If a defending player wins possession, they pass the ball to a teammate in the opposite half of the field and immediately all three defenders sprint across the midline to join their teammates.

4. Three opponents also sprint across the midline to regain possession.

5. Continue to play 5 vs 3 in each half by repeating this pattern with each change of possession.

COACHING TIPS

•   Emphasize immediate transition from attack to defense upon loss of possession.

THREE TEAM RONDO

OBJECTIVE

- To utilize passing combinations among teammates to maintain possession of the ball from opponents

SETUP

- Organize three teams of three players each.

- Teams position themselves within a 30-yard-long by 25-yard-wide area.

- Each team wears a different color scrimmage vest.

- Designate one team as the defending team to begin.

- The other two teams are attacking teams to begin.

- The coach is positioned beside the field with a supply of balls.

PROCEDURE

1. To initiate play the coach serves a ball to either of the two attacking teams.

2. The two attacking teams combine to keep the ball from the defending team, creating a 6-vs-3 player advantage for the attacking teams.

3. If the defending team wins possession of the ball, the team that lost possession immediately becomes the defenders

4. Play is continuous as teams alternate from attack to defense.

COACHING TIPS

*   Emphasize the importance of using the entire space to stretch the defending players and create passing options.

4 VS 4 + 2 TARGETS

OBJECTIVE

• To develop passing patterns among central midfield players

SETUP

• Play on a 35-yard-long by 25-yard-wide field area.

• Organize two teams of five players each.

• Each team defends an end line of the field.

• Designate one member of each team as the target player who positions on the end line defended by the opposing team.

• The remaining four players from each team position themselves within the field area.

• Award one team the ball to begin.

PROCEDURE

1. The team with possession of the ball can score a point by completing a pass to their target player stationed on the opponent's end line.

2. The defending team tries to deny passes to the opponents' target player positioned on their end line.

3. The first team to score five points wins the round.

4. Reorganize teams and repeat with a different player as the target.

COACHING TIPS

- Emphasize the importance of creating passing lanes through proper support positioning of players in the area near the ball.

RISK VS REWARD

OBJECTIVES

- To practice the appropriate use (when and where) of dribbling skills in game situations

- To improve fitness

SETUP

- Divide the group into two teams of five to seven field players plus a goalkeeper.

- Position markers to create a 45-yard-wide by 60-yard-long field with a regulation goal centered on each end line.

- Divide the field lengthwise into three 20-yard-deep by 45-yard-wide zones.

- Station a goalkeeper in each goal.

- Use colored vests to differentiate teams.

- One ball is required per game; an extra supply of balls is recommended.

PROCEDURE

1. Begin with a kickoff from the center of the field.

2. Each team defends a goal and can score in the opponents' goal.

3. Regular soccer rules are in effect except for the following restrictions:

   - Players are restricted to three or fewer touches to receive and pass the ball when in the defending third of the field nearest their goal.

   - In the middle zone, players are permitted to dribble when advancing the ball in open space but are not permitted to take on and beat (bypass) opponents on the dribble.

   - In the attacking third of the field (nearest to the opponents' goal) players are permitted to beat (bypass) an opponent by dribbling to create a scoring opportunity.

4. Violation of the zone restrictions results in a loss of possession and a free kick to the opposing team.

5. The team scoring the most goals wins the match.

COACHING TIPS

- Emphasize the fact that dribbling skills are used most effectively in the attacking third of the field, an area where the risk of possession loss is outweighed by the possibility of creating a goal-scoring opportunity.

- Encourage players to take on (dribble past) opponents in the attacking third of the field.

- Discourage excessive dribbling, particularly in the defending and middle thirds of the field, as these are areas where loss of possession often translates into scoring opportunities for the opponent.

3 VS 3 TO FOUR GOALS

OBJECTIVES

- To develop teamwork and combination play

- To practice group offensive and defensive tactics

SETUP

- Position markers to outline a field area 30 yards long by 25 yards wide.

- Place two 4-yard-wide goals an equal distance apart on each end line for a total of four goals.

- Organize teams of three players each.

- Do not use goalkeepers.

PROCEDURE

1. Two teams enter the field area to compete 3 vs 3.

2. Coach serves a ball to one of the teams to initiate play.

3. The team with possession attempts to score through either of the two goals on the opponent's end line.

4. Immediately after a shot on goal, a goal scored, or the ball out of play, the coach serves another ball into the area and play continues.

5. Play for three minutes at high intensity, then two new teams enter the area and repeat the exercise.

6. Do not use goalkeepers.

7. Continue until each team has played every other team at least once.

COACHING TIPS

• Place emphasis on immediate transition from attack to defense and vice vera on each change of possession.

FIND THE TARGET

sports-graphics.com

OBJECTIVE

- To utilize passing combinations and player movement to create passing lanes to a designated target player

SETUP

- Play within a 40-yard square area.

- Position markers to outline a 10-yard-square area located in the center of the larger area.

- Designate one player as the "target" who is positioned within the 10-yard square.

- Divide the remaining players into two teams who position themselves within the larger area but outside of the 10-yard square.

- The coach is positioned outside the playing area with a supply of balls.

PROCEDURE

1. The coach passes a ball to one of the teams within the field area to initiate play.

2. The team with possession attempts to complete a pass to the target player.

3. The opponents try to prevent passes to the target and at the same time gain possession of the ball.

4. Upon change of possession the team roles reverse.

5. The target player must stay within the 10-yard central square but can move within the square as needed to be available for a pass.

6. A pass completed to the target player counts one point.

7. After receiving a passed ball the target player immediately returns the ball to the team that scored the point and play continues.

COACHING TIPS

- The team with possession should pass the ball quickly to create passing lanes to the target player.

IN AND OUT

OBJECTIVES

- To create goal scoring opportunities through combination play

- To practice defending principles and tactics used in the area of the ball

- To provide goalkeeper practice

SETUP

- Play on one end of a regulation field with a full-sized goal on the end line.

- Double the size of the penalty area by placing a line of markers 36 yards from the goal spanning the width of the penalty area.

- The double penalty area (44 yards wide by 36 yards deep) represents the playing area.

- Organize two teams of three or four players each, plus a neutral goalkeeper in goal.

- Teams wear different colored vests and position themselves within the playing area.

- Coach is stationed outside of the field area with a supply of balls.

PROCEDURE

1. Coach initiates play by passing a ball into the area where teams compete for possession of the ball.

2. The team winning possession attacks the goal—the opponents defend.

3. After a shot at goal, a goal scored, or a change of possession, the ball is returned to the coach who immediately initiates the next round by passing the ball into the area.

4. Play is continuous as teams attack or defend depending upon who has possession of the ball.

5. The first team to score five goals wins the contest.

COACHING TIPS

- Designate a neutral player (or two) who always joins the team in possession to create a numerical player advantage for the attacking team. The neutral player does not defend.

POSSESS TO PENETRATE

sports-graphics.com

OBJECTIVE

- To create opportunities for attacking players to pass the ball forward to break lines of defense

SETUP

- Position markers to outline a 30-yard-square area divided into three 10-yard-deep zones.

- Organize three teams of four players each.

- Position a team in each of the three zones (zones 1, 2, 3).

- The team stationed in end zone 1 has the ball to begin.

- No goalkeepers are required.

PROCEDURE

1. Players stationed in end zone 1 pass the ball among themselves to create available passing lanes to pass the ball forward through zone 2 to the players in the opposite end zone (3).

2. The team (players) in the middle zone play as defenders and attempt to prevent passes through their zone.

3. All passes must be on the ground.

4. Players in the end zones are limited to three or fewer touches to pass the ball among themselves.

5. A pass that goes through the middle zone and is completed to a player in the opposite end zone is awarded one point.

6. If a player in the middle zone intercepts a pass, or the ball travels outside of the field area, the team that committed the error moves to the middle zone and becomes defenders, and the original defending team moves to an end zone.

7. Play for 15 minutes as players rotate from the center (defending) zone into the end (attacking/passing) zones upon each change of possession.

COACHING TIPS

- Emphasize ball movement, decision-making speed, and proper angles of support to create open passing lanes.

- Place emphasis on possession with the objective of penetration (passing through the middle zone).

ATTACK THE SPACE BEHIND

sports-graphics.com

OBJECTIVE

- To develop the passing combinations and teamwork required to penetrate and get behind an opponent's defensive block

SETUP

- Organize two teams of five to seven players each.

- Position markers to outline a field area 60 yards long by 50 yards wide.

- On each end of the field place markers to designate an end zone 10 yards deep spanning the width of the field.

- Assign each team an end zone to defend.

- Both teams station themselves in the central area of the field between the end zones.

- No goals or goalkeepers are required.

- Award one team the ball to begin.

PROCEDURE

1. Drill starts with a kickoff at the center of the field.

2. Basic rules apply other than the method of scoring. A team scores one point when a player completes a pass to a teammate who has moved into the opponent's end zone.

3. Players on the defending team are not permitted to enter their own end zone to intercept passes; they must collectively position themselves to block passing lanes to prevent opponent passes from entering their end zone (the space behind).

4. Change of possession occurs when the defending team wins the ball, when the ball goes out of play last touched by a member of the team in possession, or after a point is scored. Otherwise, play is continuous.

COACHING TIPS

- Adjust the field size to accommodate the ages and abilities of players.

- Smaller end zones make it more difficult to score points, and larger (deeper and wider) end zones make it more difficult for defending players to prevent scores.

4 VS 4 + TWO NEUTRALS

OBJECTIVES

- To practice attacking combinations in a numbers-up (numerical advantage of players) situation

- To practice group defending tactics in a numbers-down situation

SETUP

- Organize two teams of four players each.

- Designate two additional players as neutrals who always join the team with possession of the ball.

- Neutrals do not defend.

- Use markers to outline an area of 30 yards square.

- Both teams and the neutrals position themselves within the field area.

PROCEDURE

1. Award one team the ball to begin.

2. Neutrals join with the team in possession to create a 6-vs-4 numerical player advantage for that team as it attempts to keep possession from opponents.

3. If the defending team wins possession of the ball the two neutrals immediately join that team to create a 6-vs-4 player advantage.

4. Award a team one point for completing five or more consecutive passes without loss of possession.

5. The first team to score ten points wins the contest.

COACHING POINTS

- Encourage the team in possession to utilize the entire space to stretch the defending team and create passing lanes.

- For experienced players, institute a touch limit (three or fewer touches permitted before passing the ball).

- Violation of the touch limit results in loss of possession to the opponents.

5 VS 3 + TWO GOALKEEPERS FOUR-GOAL GAME

OBJECTIVES

- To develop the combination play required to stretch an opposing defense and attack the most vulnerable spaces

- To practice group defending tactics in an outnumbered situation

SETUP

- Position markers to create a 40-yard-long by 35-yard-wide field area.

- Organize two teams of five or six players each.

- Place a small goal (4 yards wide) at each corner of each end line for a total of four goals.

- Award one team possession of the ball to begin.

PROCEDURE

1. Each team defends the two goals on its end line and can score through either of the two goals on the opponent's end line.

2. The team with possession of the ball attacks with five players; the opponents defend with three field players.

3. The two remaining players on the defending team immediately drop back into the goals to play as goalkeepers when the team loses possession of the ball.

4. The five attacking players are limited to four or fewer touches to pass, receive, and shoot the ball.

5. A defending player who wins the ball must first pass it back to one of their two teammates playing as goalkeepers before all five players can attack the opponent's goals. This allows two players on the opposing team time to drop into the goals as goalkeepers.

6. The team in possession scores one point each time it can pass or shoot the ball to one of the opposing team's goalkeepers.

COACHING TIPS

- Emphasize immediate transition from defense to attack and vice versa upon change of possession.

- Attacking players should circulate the ball quickly to unbalance the outnumbered defenders to create open passing lanes and scoring opportunities.

- The outnumbered defending players should position themselves to protect the most critical space and force attackers to shoot from poor (wide) angles.

4 VS 2 TO 6 VS 4 RONDO

OBJECTIVE

•   To maintain possession of the ball from outnumbered opponents

SETUP

•   Position markers to outline a 20-yard-square field area.

•   Organize a team of four players, a team of two players, and designate four additional players as neutrals.

•   The team of four players and team of two players are positioned within the area.

•   Position a neutral player on each sideline of the field area.

- Neutral players are not permitted to enter the field area; they can only move laterally along their sideline to receive from and return passes to the two central players.

- One ball is required.

- Place an extra supply of balls outside the playing area in case the game ball is kicked away.

PROCEDURE

1. The four-player team attempts to maintain possession of the ball from the two-player team within the grid area.

2. If the two-player team gains possession of the ball they try to keep possession by using the four neutral players positioned on the sidelines as potential passing options, creating a 6-vs-4 situation.

3. The four-player team are not permitted to use the neutrals as potential passing options.

COACHING TIPS

- Adjust the area size to match the ages, abilities, and number of the players.

- Slide tackles should not be permitted.

SIX ATTACKERS VS FOUR DEFENDERS

OBJECTIVE

- To practice small-group tactical play for both attack and defense

SETUP

- Play on one-half of a regulation field with a full-sized goal on one end line.

- Station a goalkeeper in the full goal.

- Position two small counter-attack goals (4 yards wide) on the end line opposite the full goal.

- Do not use goalkeepers in the small goals.

- Designate a team of six players and a team of four players.

PROCEDURE

1. The six-player team attempts to score in the full goal against the four-player team and the goalkeeper.

2. The four-player team defends the full goal and can score by passing the ball through either of the two small counter-attack goals.

COACHING TIPS

*   Encourage the six-player team to use the entire field space to stretch and create gaps within their opponent's defense.

*   Encourage the four-player team to protect/control the most dangerous scoring space and force their opponents into poor shooting positions.

DRIBBLE ACROSS THE END LINE TO SCORE

OBJECTIVE

- To combine passing and dribbling skills to create penetrating runs with the ball through an opponent's defensive block

SETUP

- Play on a 30-yard-wide by 40-yard-long field.

- Organize two teams of four to six players. Each team defends an end line of the field.

- No goalkeepers required.

PROCEDURE

1. Regular soccer rules are in effect except for the method of scoring.

2. Goals are scored by dribbling the ball across the opponent's end line rather than by shooting at goal.

3. The entire length of the end line is considered the goal line.

COACHING TIPS

- Encourage players to combine with teammates to create situations where a player can dribble over the opponent's end line with control of the ball.

CHANGE THE POINT OF ATTACK

OBJECTIVE

- To quickly change the location of the ball (point of attack) to unbalance the defending team and attack the most vulnerable space (goal)

SETUP

- Place markers to outline a field area 35 yards long by 25 yards wide.

- Place three small goals, each 4 yards wide, an equal distance apart on each end line of the field for a total of six goals.

- Organize two teams of four or five players each.

- Each team defends the three goals on its end line and can score by passing the ball through any of the three goals on the opponent's end line.

- Do not use goalkeepers.

PROCEDURE

1. Coach initiates play by serving a ball into the field area.

2. The team gaining possession attempts to score; their opponents defend.

3. Teams transition from attack to defense and vice versa on each change of possession.

COACHING TIPS

• Emphasize the importance of moving the ball quickly to unbalance defenders and create open passing/shooting lanes to the goals.

SMALL GROUP ATTACK AND DEFEND

sports-graphics.com

OBJECTIVE

- To practice immediate transition from attack to defense and vice versa upon change of possession

SETUP

- Organize two teams (1 and 2) of six players each, plus goalkeepers.

- Play on a 30-yard-long by 20-yard-wide field with a full-sized goal centered on each end line (goals A and B).

- Station a goalkeeper in each goal.

- Use colored vests to differentiate teams.

- Position both teams on the same end line of the field, one team to each side of goal A.

- In preparation to begin the drill, two players from team 2 position themselves to defend goal B.

- Place a supply of balls beside each goal.

- Team 1 has the ball to begin.

PROCEDURE

1. Three players from team 1 advance off the end line to attack goal B, defended by two players from team 2 and a goalkeeper.

2. Immediately after a shot on goal, a shot traveling over the end line, or a ball won by a defender, the goalkeeper in goal B distributes the ball to the two original defenders (team 2), who immediately attack goal A.

3. One of the three original attackers from team 1 positions to defend goal A, creating a 2-vs-1 player advantage for team 2 as they counterattack on goal A.

4. The other two original attackers from team 1 remain near goal B to defend against team 2 in the next round.

5. Immediately after an attempt on goal A, three players from team 2 advance off the line to attack goal B, which is now defended by two players from team 1.

6. The game continues back and forth, with teams attacking goal B 3 vs 2 and counterattacking goal A 2 vs 1.

7. The team scoring the most goals is the winner.

COACHING TIPS

- Emphasize immediate transition from attack to defense and vice versa.

ATTACK NUMBERS UP—DEFEND NUMBERS DOWN

sports-graphics.com

OBJECTIVES

- To practice attack and defense tactics in a 3-vs-2 situation

- To provide goalkeeper training

SETUP

- Organize two teams of five field players plus a goalkeeper.

- Play on a 30-yard-wide by 40-yard-long field area, bisected by a midline.

- Position a regulation goal on each end line of the field.

- For each team designate three attackers who position themselves in the opponent's half of the field.

- Designate two players on each team as defenders, who are positioned in their team's half of the field to defend their goal.

- This setup creates a 3-vs-2 player advantage for the attacking team in each half of the field.

- Use colored vests to differentiate teams.

- One ball is required per game. Place an extra supply of balls near each goal.

PROCEDURE

1. Award one team possession of the ball to kickoff.

2. Each team defends a goal and can score on the opponent's goal.

3. Players are restricted to movement within their assigned half of the field.

4. If a defending player wins possession of the ball they must pass it to a teammate stationed in the opponent's half of the field to initiate a counterattack on the opponent's goal.

5. A shot on goal saved by the goalkeeper can be distributed directly to a teammate stationed in the opponent's half of the field.

6. Play is continuous as teams defend 2 vs 3 and attack 3 vs 2.

7. The team scoring the most goals wins.

COACHING TIPS

- Zonal defensive concepts apply as defending players are outnumbered in their half of the field.

- One defender should pressure the opponent on the ball, while the second defender is positioned to provide cover for the first defender.

- Defenders should reposition quickly in response to movement of the opponents to reduce available passing options.

- Encourage the attacking team to use quick passing combinations to take advantage of the numerical player advantage in the opponent's half of the field.

TARGET PRACTICE

OBJECTIVE

*   To develop passing combinations to combine with a specific target player

SETUP

*   Position markers to outline a field area of 35 yards long and 25 yards wide.

*   Organize teams of six players each.

*   Designate one player on each team as a target who wears a distinctive colored training vest.

*   The coach is positioned outside of the field area with a supply of balls.

PROCEDURE

1. The coach initiates play by passing a ball into the field area.

2. The team that gains possession attempts to keep the ball and complete a pass to their target player who is free to move throughout the area.

3. When the target player receives a pass from a teammate then he or she must complete a pass to a different teammate in order to score one point.

4. The opposing team attempts to gain possession of the ball and at the same time deny passes to their opponent's target player.

5. If the ball travels outside the field area the coach immediately passes another ball into the field area and play continues.

6. Play for 15 minutes and keep score.

7. The team totaling the most points wins the competition.

COACHING TIPS

•   Encourage teammates to circulate the ball quickly and keep passes on the ground.

•   For more experienced players, limit the number of touches permitted to receive and pass the ball.

DIRECTIONAL RONDO

OBJECTIVE

- To maintain possession of the ball while penetrating the opponent's half of the field

SETUP

- Play on a 35-yard-wide by 50-yard-long field area.

- Organize two teams of six players each.

- Each team defends an end line of the field; there are no goals.

- One player from each team positions on the opponent's end line as the target.

- The remaining players (five for each team) position themselves in the center of the playing area to compete with their opponents.

- Designate two additional players as neutrals who always join the team in possession of the ball to create a 7-vs-5 player advantage for the attacking team.

- Teams wear different colors and neutral players wear distinctive colored vests.

PROCEDURE

1. Award one team possession of the ball for kickoff at midfield.

2. Each team defends an end line and can score by completing a pass to their target player who is positioned on the opponent's end line.

3. A pass completed to the team's target player scores one point.

4. The player who completes a pass to the target player takes his or her place on the end line and becomes the target.

5. The original target becomes a field player and play continues.

6. The first team to score five goals wins the game.

COACHING TIPS

- Encourage players to circulate the ball quickly with the majority of passes on the ground.

- For more experienced players limit the number of touches permitted to receive and pass the ball.

4 VS 4 + FOUR PERIMETER PLAYERS

OBJECTIVES

• To rehearse attacking combinations used to provide service from wide areas

• To finish crosses

SETUP

• Play on a 50-yard-long by 40-yard-wide field area, divided lengthwise by a midline.

• Position a regulation-sized goal on each end line.

• Organize two teams of eight players each, plus goalkeepers.

• Teams are differentiated by colored scrimmage vests.

PROCEDURE

1. Four players from each team position themselves within the field area to create a 4-vs-4 situation within the field.

2. The remaining four players from each team station themselves along the perimeter lines in the opponent's half of the field.

3. One player is positioned on each touchline (sideline) and one player is positioned on each side of the goal along the end line.

4. Perimeter players may combine (pass) with their teammates who are competing within the field but are limited to two touches to receive and pass the ball when doing so.

5. Perimeter players may not enter the field area and are not permitted to pass the ball to one another; they can only pass and receive the ball with their teammates who are competing within the field area.

6. Perimeter players positioned on the touchlines (sidelines) are encouraged to serve crosses into the goal area when possible.

7. Perimeter players who are positioned on the end lines are encouraged to redirect a ball passed to them into area in front of goal for a teammate to finish.

8. Teams defend with the four central players only.

9. The four perimeter players are inactive until their team gains possession and advances the ball into the opponent's half of the field.

10. With every two goals scored, the teams' four perimeter players switch roles with their four central teammates and play continues.

COACHING TIPS

- Encourage players to use their sideline and end line perimeter teammates to create an 8-vs-4 player advantage when in possession of the ball.

- Perimeter players should serve crosses into the goal area, when possible, to create game-simulated scoring opportunities.

PROMOTION VS RELEGATION

OBJECTIVE

- To practice attacking and defending tactics used in a small-group situation

SETUP

- Use markers to outline two 30-by-20-yard fields laid out side by side, with a 10-yard space between fields.

- Designate one field as the promotion field, and the other as the relegation field.

- Place a small goal (4-yards wide) on both end lines of each field.

- Organize teams of three or four players each, and number the teams 1 through 4.

- Pair team 1 with team 4 and team 2 with team 3 for the first game of the tournament.

- No goalkeepers required.

PROCEDURE

1. The first games (1 vs 4 and 2 vs 3) begin at the same time but on different fields.

2. Each game is 10 minutes in duration; the coach keeps time.

3. Goals are scored by passing/shooting the ball through the opponent's goal.

4. Defending players are not permitted to station themselves in the goals as goalkeepers—there are no goalkeepers in this drill.

5. The winning teams on each field are promoted to play against each other on the promotion field in the next round of play, while the losing teams are relegated to play one another on the relegation field in the next round of play.

6. Play a total of four or five games.

7. The team winning the most games is the champion.

COACHING TIPS

- Emphasize immediate transition from attack to defense upon change of possession.

SECTION 7 GOALKEEPING

Much like goalkeepers in the sports of hockey and lacrosse, the soccer goalkeeper is a specialist and must be trained as such. The goalkeeper is the only member of the team permitted use of the hands to receive and control balls directed at the goal by opponents. She or he must be competent in securing powerful shots arriving on the ground and through the air. The keeper must also be willing and able to vault through the air to make the big save or dive at the feet of an onrushing opponent to smother a breakaway. That said, the goalkeeper is not permitted to use the hands to receive and control the ball in all situations. The official laws of the game state that the goalkeeper must receive balls *passed to him or her from a teammate* with the feet (not the hands), so the keeper must be adept at performing the basic foot skills commonly used by field players to pass and receive the ball. The drills described in section 3 can be incorporated into goalkeeper training to accomplish that aim.

From a tactical standpoint the goalkeeper should acquire a basic understanding of angle play in order to position to best advantage when preparing to make a save. And, after making the save, the goalkeeper is responsible for initiating a counter-attack by distributing the ball accurately to a teammate. This is usually accomplished by throwing or rolling the ball, although in some cases it involves the use of foot skills to pass the ball to a teammate who can then initiate the counterattack.

The ball-handling drills described in section 7 provide fundamental exercises that introduce aspiring goalkeepers to the techniques used when diving, saving, and securing shots at goal. These drills can be used as a lead-up to more intense training for older, physically mature goalkeepers.

IMPORTANT NOTE ON GOALKEEPING

Players under 12 years of age should not, as a general rule, specialize solely in the goalkeeper position. It is important for all players, even those who feel they may ultimately want to play as a goalkeeper, to develop the fundamental foot skills used by field players. The constantly evolving role of the goalkeeper requires that he or she be able to perform passing and receiving foot skills much more so today than in the past.

SHUFFLE, TOSS, AND CATCH

OBJECTIVES

- To develop confidence in receiving and catching the ball

- To develop "soft" hands

SETUP

- Goalkeepers pair with a partner and stand approximately 5 yards apart facing one another.

- Each keeper holds a ball in their right hand at approximately head height.

PROCEDURE

1. Partners slowly shuffle sideways while facing one another (do not cross legs when shuffling sideways).

2. While doing so they simultaneously toss the ball from their right hand to their partner's left hand.

3. Tosses are received with one hand only.

4. The ball is returned by tossing with the left hand to the partner's right hand.

5. Partners continue shuffling sideways for 20 yards, then reverse direction and repeat.

6. Assess one penalty point for each time a goalkeeper drops the ball.

7. Keeper who accumulates the fewest number of points wins the competition.

COACHING TIPS

• Keepers should withdraw the hand as the ball arrives to soften the impact.

SCOOP SAVE THE LOW SHOT

sports-graphics.com

OBJECTIVE

• To practice collecting and securing rolling (ground) balls

SETUP

• Goalkeeper A faces two teammates (goalkeepers B and C) at a distance of 10 yards.

• Goalkeeper B has the ball to begin.

PROCEDURE

1. Goalkeeper B rolls a ball with firm pace toward A and sprints to A's position.

2. Goalkeeper A uses the scoop save technique to collect the ball, allowing it to roll up on the forearms and clutching it to chest.

3. Goalkeeper A immediately rolls the ball to goalkeeper C and sprints to that position.

   • Goalkeeper C receives the ball and rolls it to B and sprints to that position.

   • Continue the drill for two minutes so that each goalkeeper makes multiple scoop saves.

COACHING TIPS

• The scoop technique allows the ball to roll up over the hands and onto the forearms, then it is clutched to chest.

• The ball is not received directly onto the hands.

SIDE SHUFFLE AND SAVE

sports-graphics.com

OBJECTIVE

- To collect low shots directed at the goal

SETUP

- The goalkeeper is positioned in goal near to one goal post.

- Three servers, each with a ball, position themselves facing the goalkeeper at 10 to 12 yards of distance.

- One server is positioned in line with each goal post, while the third server is positioned front and center of the goal.

PROCEDURE

1. On coach command the goalkeeper begins slowly shuffling sideways across the goal mouth.

2. Each server, in turn, passes a rolling ball toward the goalkeeper.

3. The goalkeeper uses the scoop save to secure the ball, tosses it back to the server, and continues to the next server.

4. The goalkeeper continues to shuffle back and forth across the goal receiving and securing rolling balls using the scoop save technique.

5. Continue for two minutes.

6. Rest 30 seconds, then repeat.

COACHING TIPS

- The scoop technique allows the ball to roll up over the hands, onto the forearms, and then is clutched to chest.

CATCH AND HOLD

OBJECTIVE

- To catch and hold powerful point-blank shots

SETUP

- Goalkeeper pairs with a partner.

- Partners face one another at approximately 6 to 8 yards.

- One goalkeeper has the ball.

- Place an extra ball beside each goalkeeper in case the original ball is kicked away.

PROCEDURE

1. Partners volley a ball out of their hands back and forth to one another.

2. All volleys should be struck with power and aimed at the partner's chest or head.

3. The keeper attempts to catch and hold the ball, then returns it by volleying to the partner.

4. Award one point for each volley shot caught and held, without dropping the ball to the ground.

5. Repeat for 20 shots at each partner.

6. The keeper totaling the most points wins the competition.

COACHING TIPS

*   The ball should be received on the fingertips and palms with hands and head behind the ball.

*   Palms face forward with fingers spread and slightly extended.

*   Withdraw hands upon contact with the ball to cushion the impact.

*   Position the body behind the ball as it arrives, to serve as a barrier.

GOALIE WARS

OBJECTIVE

- To improve shot-saving ability

SETUP

- Goalkeepers (A and B) partner for shot-stopping competition.

- Position markers to outline a 25-yard-long field area with a full-sized goal on each end line.

- The goalkeepers position themselves in opposite goals.

- Keeper A has the ball to begin.

- Place several extra balls in each goal.

PROCEDURE

1. Keeper A takes up to four steps forward of the goal line and attempts to volley or throw the ball past goalkeeper B into the goal.

2. Keeper B may move forward off the goal line to narrow the shooting angle.

3. After a save, or goal scored, keeper B attempts to score against A in the same manner.

4. Keepers return to their respective goal line after each shot on goal.

5. Award two points for a ball caught and held, and one point for a save made by parrying the ball wide or over the goal.

6. The keeper who totals the most points wins the war.

COACHING TIPS

- Goalkeepers should move forward off the goal line to narrow the shooter's angle.

- If the goalkeeper is not confident of holding the ball he or she should deflect (parry) it out of play.

SAVE THE BREAKAWAY

sports-graphics.com

OBJECTIVE

• To save in a breakaway situation

SETUP

• Goalkeepers (A and B) partner for shot-saving competition.

• Place markers to outline a field that is 25 yards long by 20 yards wide.

• Place a full-sized goal, or flags to represent a full-sized goal, on each end line.

• Goalkeepers station themselves in opposite goals.

• Goalkeeper A has the ball to begin.

PROCEDURE

1. Goalkeeper A dribbles at goalkeeper B and attempts to score by dribbling past or passing the ball underneath B, simulating a breakaway situation.

2. Keeper B moves forward from the goal line to make a save.

3. After each attempt (save or goal scored) the goalkeepers return to their respective goals and repeat the round in the opposite direction.

4. Goalkeepers switch from attack (dribbler) to defense (goalkeeper) every other round.

5. Award one point for each save of a breakaway situation.

6. The goalkeeper who totals the most points (saves) wins the competition.

COACHING TIPS

*   Encourage the keeper to move forward from the goal line to narrow the shooting angle and present a larger barrier to the dribbler.

*   Emphasize the importance of balance and body control.

*   As the keeper advances from the goal line he or she should shift into a semi-crouched posture with knees bent and arms extended downward to sides.

*   To make the save the keeper should go down on the side (not head first) with arms and hands extended toward the ball.

SET AND SAVE

sports-graphics.com

OBJECTIVES

- To improve angle play

- To provide shot-saving practice

SETUP

- Play on one end of a regulation field.

- Position markers to represent four small gates, each 2 yards wide, spread along the front of the penalty area.

- Place a gate at each corner at the front edge of the penalty area and a gate on each side of the penalty arc.

- Station a player (shooter) with two soccer balls behind each gate.

- The goalkeeper is positioned in the goal.

PROCEDURE

1. Shooters, in turn, dribble through their respective gate and shoot on goal from 15 yards of distance or greater.

2. Goalkeeper should advance off the line to narrow the shooting angle and make the save.

3. After each shot or save, the goalkeeper returns to the goal line, sets in the ready position, and prepares to save the next shot.

4. Each shooter takes two shots, for a total of eight shots for each round.

5. Repeat with a different goalkeeper in goal.

6. Play at least three rounds for each goalkeeper.

COACHING TIPS

- Emphasize proper footwork and optimal positioning to reduce the shooter's angle to goal.

- The keeper should get in position and set (not move) the feet just prior to release of the shot.

PIN THE ROLLING (GROUND) BALL

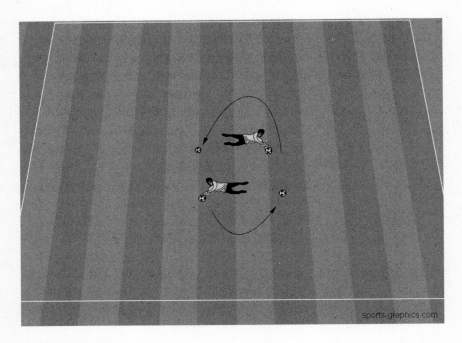

sports-graphics.com

OBJECTIVE

- To improve the technique used to dive and secure a low shot to either side

SETUP

- Two goalkeepers kneel facing one another at 2–3 yards.
- Place a ball 1 yard to the right and 1 yard to the left of each goalkeeper.

PROCEDURE

1. On command both goalkeepers fall sideways (dive) to their left and pin the ball to the ground, with one hand behind the ball and one on top of the ball.

2. After making the save the keepers immediately return to kneeling posture and fall to their right to pin the ball to the ground.

3. Continue for 45 seconds, relax, then repeat.

COACHING TIPS

- Encourage goalkeepers to pin the ball and immediately reset to make the next save.

- To make the drill more challenging have the keepers pin a rolling ball from a squatting position.

DIVE OR SMOTHER TO SAVE

sports-graphics.com

OBJECTIVE

* To provide the goalkeeper with shot-save training

SETUP

* Position markers to outline a field 40 yards long and 25 yards wide.

* Divided the field lengthwise by a midline.

* Position a full-sized goal on each end line.

* Organize two teams of four to six players and a goalkeeper.

* Goalkeepers are positioned in opposite goals.

* The goalkeeper's teammates, each with a ball, line up at the goal post to their goalkeeper's right, facing the opponents stationed on the opposite end line.

PROCEDURE

1. On the coach's command the first player from each team attacks (dribbles at) the opponent's goalkeeper.

2. When the dribbler crosses the midline of the field he or she has the option to shoot on goal or continue to dribble forward to beat the goalkeeper on a breakaway.

3. Immediately after each save or score the next player in line attempts to score in the same manner.

4. Continue until each field player has attempted to score on the opposing goalkeeper.

5. Reorganize teams and repeat for several rounds.

6. The goalkeeper conceding the fewest goals wins the competition.

COACHING TIPS

*   The goalkeeper should narrow the shooting angle by moving forward off the goal line.

*   The keeper should maintain balance and body control when advancing off the goal line.

RAPID FIRE SET AND SAVE

OBJECTIVE

- To improve goalkeeper ability to make saves of point-blank shots

SETUP

- Play on one end of a regulation field with a full-sized goal.

- Goalkeepers (A and B) partner for competition.

- Four to six field players (shooters), each with a ball, position themselves at various spots within the penalty area, all within 12 to 15 yards of the goal.

- Label each shooter with a number, beginning with 1 and up through the number of shooters.

- Goalkeeper A is positioned in goal for the first round of shots.

PROCEDURE

1. On the coach command player 1 shoots to score, and the keeper attempts to save.

2. Shooter 2 immediately follows suit, then shooter 3, and so on up through the number of shooters.

3. Shots are taken in rapid succession so the goalkeeper must assume the set position, save, and immediately reset to make the next save.

4. Play a total of five rounds for each goalkeeper.

5. The goalkeeper who concedes the fewest goals wins the competition.

COACHING TIPS

• Encourage goalkeepers to save and then immediately reset to make the next save.

• Goalkeepers do not have to hold the ball, but merely parry it wide of the goal to make the save.

LOW-BALL TRAINING

OBJECTIVE

- To save and hold low-driven shots using the forward vault technique

SETUP

- Pair goalkeepers (A and B) for competition.

- Place markers to outline a 15-yard-wide by 20-yard-long field area.

- Position additional markers to represent a 6-yard-wide goal on each end line.

- Goalkeepers are stationed in opposite goals.

- Goalkeeper A has the ball to begin.

PROCEDURE

1. Goalkeeper A advances out from the goal and throws the ball so that it bounces (skips) off the ground directly in front of goalkeeper B.

2. Goalkeeper B attempts to save using the forward vault technique with forearms slipped beneath the ball and the ball clutched to the chest.

3. If goalkeeper B fails to hold the ball, then keeper A may follow up the shot and score off the rebound.

4. After each save or goal, keepers return to their respective goals and repeat the drill in the opposite direction.

5. Continue for a predetermined number of shots.

6. Award one point for a ball held without rebound.

7. The goalkeeper who scores the most points wins the competition.

COACHING TIPS

- The goalkeeper should align with the oncoming ball and dive forward to smother the shot, clutching the ball between forearms and chest.

- Elbows and arms should be cradled underneath the ball to prevent it from bouncing free.

- Goalkeepers should not try to catch the low skipping shot directly in their hands, as this increases the risk of a rebound. The ball should be secured to the chest with forearms.

HIGH-BALL TRAINING

OBJECTIVE

- To improve the technique used to receive a high ball served into the goal area

SETUP

- Play on one end of a field with a regulation goal.

- The goalkeeper is positioned on the goal line in the center of the goal.

- Two servers (1 and 2), each with a ball, are positioned just outside of the 18-yard box, one server on each side of the penalty area.

PROCEDURE

1. Server 1 tosses (or volleys) a ball above the height of the crossbar so that it will drop within the 6-yard box.

2. The goalkeeper advances off the goal line, catches the ball at the highest point of his or her jump, and secures it to the chest.

3. The keeper returns the ball to the server, repositions on the goal line, and repeats the drill with server 2 tossing or volleying the high ball.

4. Continue for at least twenty receptions by the goalkeeper, alternating from one side and then the other.

COACHING TIPS

*   Encourage the keeper to extend arms and hands upward to receive the ball at the highest possible point of the jump.

DOMINATE THE BOX

OBJECTIVE

- To provide goalkeeper training for handling a variety of air balls served into the goal area

SETUP

- Organize two groups of three servers.

- Position markers to outline a field area of 40 yards wide by 50 yards long, divided lengthwise by a midline.

- Position a full-sized goal with goalkeeper on each end line.

- Three servers (each with a ball) are positioned on opposite end lines, at the corner of the field to the goalkeeper's right.

PROCEDURE

1. The first server on both ends of the field, at the same time, dribbles forward along the touchline (sideline) toward the opposite goal and at the appropriate moment serves a high lofted ball into the goal area.

2. The goalkeeper advances off the goal line to collect the ball, then returns (distributes) the ball to the player who crossed the ball into the goal area.

3. The player who crossed the ball into the goal mouth then joins the line of servers on that end of the field who repeat the drill in the opposite direction.

4. Immediately after the goalkeepers receives the ball, the next server (on both ends of the field) repeats the action.

5. Continue until each goalkeeper has received 15 to 20 crosses.

6. At that point reverse the direction of the dribblers and repeat for 15 to 20 crosses.

COACHING TIPS

• Keepers should attempt to receive the ball at the highest point of their jump with arms extended upward.

ONE GOALKEEPER, TWO GOALS

sports-graphics.com

OBJECTIVE

- To develop shot-saving ability; to improve mobility and footwork

SETUP

- Organize two teams of four field players and a goalkeeper.

- Use colored vests to differentiate teams.

- Place markers to outline a 40-yard-square field area.

- Position four additional markers (flags) in the center of the area to form an 8-by-8-yard square.

- Each side of the square represents a full-sized (8-yard wide) goal.

- One ball is required; place an extra supply of balls inside the square goal.

- Award one team the ball to begin.

PROCEDURE

1. The drill begins with a throw-in from outside of the playing area.

2. Each team is responsible for defending two adjacent sides of the square goal and can score through the other (opponent's) two sides of the square.

3. The goalkeepers for each team must defend both of their team's goals.

4. Shots can be taken from any distance and any angle.

5. Goalkeepers should use the side shuffle when moving from one goal to the adjacent goal in response to movement of the ball.

6. Play for 15 to 20 minutes.

7. The goalkeeper allowing the fewest goals wins the match.

COACHING TIPS

- Goalkeepers use the side shuffle foot movement when moving laterally to position for a save, and when moving from one goal to another.

- Goalkeepers should not cross their legs when moving laterally.

FUNDAMENTAL DIVING

OBJECTIVE

• To improve diving technique

SETUP

• Organize groups of three players (two servers and a goalkeeper).

• The servers, each with a ball, are positioned side by side facing the goalkeeper at 5 yards of distance.

• The goalkeeper assumes the ready position with knees slightly flexed and body square with the servers.

• Hands are held at approximately chest height with palms facing forward.

PROCEDURE

1. Server 1 tosses a ball to the keeper's side, at about waist height.

2. The keeper dives sideways, parallel to the ground, catches the ball, and falls to the ground on his or her side.

3. The keeper returns the ball to the server, and immediately assumes the ready position in preparation for the next save.

4. Sever 2 tosses a ball to the goalkeeper's opposite side and the keeper dives to make the save.

5. Continue at speed for 45 seconds, alternating saves from one side to the other.

6. Rest and then repeat.

COACHING TIPS

• Conduct this drill on a soft field surface, preferably grass.

SAVE, SET, AND SAVE AGAIN

OBJECTIVES

- To provide goalkeeper training to save a shot on goal and then reposition quickly to make another save and then another

- To provide field player training to score from free kicks

SETUP

- Play on one end of a field with a full-sized goal on the end line.

- The goalkeeper is positioned in the goal.

- Place eight to ten soccer balls a yard or two apart on the front edge of the penalty area, 18 yards from goal.

- Station four players 25 yards from goal as shooters.

PROCEDURE

1. Shooters take turns sprinting forward and striking a stationary ball on goal.

2. As soon as one player shoots the next shooter begins his or her approach to a ball.

3. The goalkeeper should have just enough time to make a save, then reposition to save the next shot.

4. Continue at rapid pace until the supply of balls is exhausted.

COACHING TIPS

*   Reduce the shooting distance for younger players.

PENALTY KICK COMPETITION

sports-graphics.com

OBJECTIVES

- To provide goalkeeper training to save penalty kicks

- To develop field player ability to score from penalty kicks

SETUP

- Play on one end of a field with a full-sized goal on the end line.

- The goalkeeper is positioned in the goal.

- Place a marker on the goal line one yard inside each goal post.

- Place a marker 12 yards from and center of goal to represent the penalty spot.

- Divide the group into two teams of four field players (shooters), each team with a goalkeeper.

PROCEDURE

1. Shooters alternate taking a penalty kick against the opposing goalkeeper.

2. In accordance with FIFA rules, the goalkeeper must have both feet touching the goal line and cannot move forward off the goal line until the ball is kicked.

3. Each shooter attempts five penalty kicks.

4. Award a shooter two points for a shot that beats the goalkeeper and travels within one yard of either goal post.

5. Award shooter one point for a shot that bests the keeper in the central area of the goal.

6. The goalkeeper conceding the fewest points wins the competition.

COACHING TIPS

- The goalkeeper should look for subtle hints as to where the shooter plans to aim the shot.

- The shooter should focus on keeping the shot low (below the crossbar) and on goal.

SCORE BY BREAKAWAYS ONLY

sports-graphics.com

OBJECTIVES

- To provide goalkeeper training to save breakaway opportunities

- To provide field player training as to how to beat the goalkeeper in a breakaway situation

SETUP

- Organize two teams of four field players and a goalkeeper.

- Position markers to outline 30-yard-wide by 45-yard-long field area with a full-sized goal on each end line.

- Place markers to divide the field lengthwise into three 15-yard zones.

- Station both teams in the middle zone and a goalkeeper in each goal.

- Award one team possession of the ball to begin.

PROCEDURE

1. Begin with a kickoff from the center of the field.

2. The team in possession can score only on a breakaway situation either by dribbling into or passing the ball into the opponent's defensive zone.

3. Defending players may not enter the zone nearest to their goal before the ball enters the zone carried by an opponent on the dribble or by an opponent's passed ball.

4. This restriction forces the goalkeeper to control the entire defensive zone and potentially exposes him or her to a variety of breakaway situations.

COACHING TIPS

- Adjust the field size to accommodate the age and ability of the players involved.

RAPID-FIRE LOW BALLS

OBJECTIVES

- To provide goalkeeper training to save a low shot to either side

- To reposition quickly after making a save

SETUP

- Play on one end of a field with a full-sized goal on the end line.

- The goalkeeper is positioned in the goal.

- Place six soccer balls 2 yards apart front and center of the goal, about 12 yards from the goal.

- The coach acts as the server/shooter.

PROCEDURE

1. The coach passes/shoots a ground (rolling) ball toward the corner of the goal.

2. The keeper dives to that side, pins the ball, and immediately returns to an upright position.

3. As soon as the keeper is set the coach passes a low ball to the opposite side of the goal.

4. The keeper shuffles sideways, dives to that side, pins the ball, then returns to a standing position in preparation to make the next save.

5. Continue at rapid pace until the supply of balls is exhausted.

COACHING TIPS

- Provide the goalkeeper just enough time to return to standing position before serving the next ball.

REACTION SAVES

OBJECTIVE

- To save point-blank shots to either side

SETUP

- Play on one end of a field with a full-sized goal on the end line.

- The goalkeeper is positioned in the goal.

- The coach is positioned 10 yards front and center of the goal with a supply of six to eight balls.

PROCEDURE

1. The coach throws (or volleys) a ball toward the corner of the goal that bounces about 2 yards from the goal line.

2. The keeper dives to that side, parries the ball wide of the goal, and immediately returns to an upright position.

3. As soon as the keeper is set in the upright position the coach repeats the point-blank bouncing shot the opposite side of the goal.

4. The keeper dives to that side, parries the ball wide of the goal, and returns to a standing position in preparation to make the next save.

5. Continue at rapid pace until the supply of balls is exhausted.

COACHING TIPS

- Provide the goalkeeper just enough time to return to standing position before serving the next ball.

DISTRIBUTION CIRCUIT

OBJECTIVE

- To provide goalkeeper training for distributing the ball to a teammate after making a save

SETUP

- Play on one half of a field with a full-sized goal on the end line.

- Two goalkeepers compete against one another for accuracy of distribution.

- One goalkeeper is positioned in the goal.

- His/her competitor stands beside the goal.

- Place markers to represent a 10-yard square just outside of each side of the penalty area. A player (target) is stationed within each square.

- Place additional markers to outline a 10-yard square area adjacent to each touchline 35 yards from the end line.

- A player (target) is stationed within each square.

- One player (target) is also stationed within the center circle of the field.

- The coach (server) is positioned with a supply of balls 30 yards front and center of the goal.

PROCEDURE

1. The coach serves a ball to the goalkeeper.

2. The keeper receives the ball and distributes it by rolling (or passing) the ball to a player stationed within one of the squares on the sidelines of the penalty area.

3. Repeat the drill to the square on opposite side of the penalty area.

4. The coach then serves a ball to the goalkeeper who uses the throwing technique to distribute the ball to a player in one of the squares 35 yards from the end line. Repeat the drill to the opposite side.

5. The coach then serves a ball to the goalkeeper who distributes by punting or dropkicking the ball to the player stationed in the center circle.

6. Award the goalkeeper one point for each ball distributed accurately into the designed areas.

7. Repeat the circuit five times for each goalkeeper for a total of 25 possible distribution points.

COACHING TIPS

- The goalkeeper totaling the most points wins the competition.

ABOUT THE AUTHOR

Joseph A. Luxbacher has more than three decades of experience in highly competitive athletics. He holds a PhD in Health, Physical and Recreation Education from the University of Pittsburgh. A former professional player in the North American Soccer League (NASL) and Major Indoor Soccer League (MISL), he still holds the University of Pittsburgh men's soccer scoring records for most career goals, most career points, most hat tricks, and most goals scored in one game. Upon his graduation from university, Luxbacher was recipient of the prestigious Panther Award given to the senior athlete who most promotes and sponsors the best interests of Pitt athletics.

Luxbacher has earned the "A" Coaching License of US Soccer and is a member of the United Soccer Coaches Association. He served as head men's soccer coach at the University of Pittsburgh from 1985 to 2015 when he retired from collegiate coaching. Under his charge, his Pitt teams won more than 200 games in Division I soccer. Coach Luxbacher was twice selected as Big East Athletic Conference Soccer Coach of the Year. He has authored more than a dozen books and numerous articles on the topics of soccer and peak athletic performance. His various soccer books have sold more than 250,000 copies and have been translated into several languages. He has contributed to several other books, including the college text *Introduction to Kinesiology* (5th edition), and the *Men's Health Guide to Peak Conditioning* (Rodale Press). Luxbacher has also written and produced a DVD coaching series titled "Winning Soccer" for sportvideos.com.

Luxbacher is an inductee into the Beadling Sports Club Soccer Hall of Fame, the Upper St. Clair High School Athletic Hall of Fame, the Western Pennsylvania Sports Hall of Fame, and, most recently, the University of Pittsburgh Athletic Hall of Fame (2023). He has also been honored as a Letterman of Distinction by the University of Pittsburgh. He lives in southwest Pennsylvania with wife Gail, daughter Eliza, son Travis, and dog Winston.